TAKING CARE OF YOUR SMILE

A Teen's Guide to Dental Care

D1530474

The Science of Health: Youth and Well-Being

Taking Care of Your Smile

A Teen's Guide to Dental Care

by Autumn Libal and
Christopher Hovius

Mason Crest Publishers

Philadelphia

Mason Crest Publishers Inc.
370 Reed Road, Broomall, Pennsylvania 19008
(866) MCP-BOOK (toll free)
www.masoncrest.com

ISBN 1-59084-840-3 (series)

Library of Congress Cataloging-in-Publication Data

Libal, Autumn.
 Taking care of your smile : a teen's guide to dental care / by Autumn Libal & Christopher Hovius.
     p. cm. — (The science of health)
 Includes bibliographical references and index.
 ISBN 1-59084-846-2
 1. Dental care—Juvenile literature 2. Teeth—Care and hygiene—Ju-venile literature. 3.   Dentistry—Juvenile literature.   I. Hovius, Christopher. II. Title. III. Series.
 RK63.L525 2004
 617.6'01—dc22
                                 2004002296
First edition, 2005
13 12 11 10 09 08 07 06 05   10 9 8 7 6 5 4 3 2

Designed and produced by Harding House Publishing Service, Vestal, NY 13850.
Cover design by Benjamin Stewart.
Printed and bound in India.

This book is meant to educate and should not be used as an alterna-tive to appropriate medical care. Its creators have made every effort to ensure that the information presented is accurate and up to date—but this book is not intended to substitute for the help and services of trained medical professionals.

CONTENTS

INTRODUCTION
by Dr. Sara Forman

You're not a little kid anymore. When you look in the mirror, you probably see a new person, someone who's taller, bigger, with a face that's starting to look more like an adult's than a child's. And the changes you're experiencing on the inside may be even more intense than the ones you see in the mirror. Your emotions are changing, your attitudes are changing, and even the way you think is changing. Your friends are probably more important to you than they used to be, and you no longer expect your parents to make all your decisions for you. You may be asking more questions and posing more challenges to the adults in your life. You might experiment with new identities—new ways of dressing, hairstyles, ways of talking—as you try to determine just who you really are. Your body is maturing sexually, giving you a whole new set of confusing and exciting feelings. Sorting out what is right and wrong for you may seem overwhelming.

Growth and development during adolescence is a multifaceted process involving every aspect of your being. It all happens so fast that it can be confusing and distressing. But this stage of your life is entirely normal. Every adult in your life made it through adolescence—and you will too.

7

But what exactly is adolescence? According to the American Heritage Dictionary, adolescence is "the period of physical and psychological development from the onset of puberty to maturity." What does this really mean?

In essence, adolescence is the time in our lives when the needs of childhood give way to the responsibilities of adulthood. According to psychologist Erik Erikson, these years are a time of separation and individuation. In other words, you are separating from your parents, becoming an individual in your own right. These are the years when you begin to make decisions on your own. You are becoming more self-reliant and less dependent on family members.

When medical professionals look at what's happening physically—what they refer to as the biological model—they define the teen years as a period of hormonal transformation toward sexual maturity, as well as a time of peak growth, second only to the growth during the months of infancy. This physical transformation from childhood to adulthood takes place under the influence of society's norms and social pressures; at the same time your body is changing, the people around you are expecting new things from you. This is what makes adolescence such a unique and challenging time.

Being a teenager in North America today is exciting yet stressful. For those who work with teens, whether by parenting them, educating them, or providing services to them, adolescence can be challenging as well. Youth are struggling with many messages from society and the media about how they should behave and who they should be. "Am I normal?" and "How do I fit in?" are often questions with which teens wrestle. They are facing decisions about their health such as how to take care of

8

their bodies, whether to use drugs and alcohol, or whether to have sex.

This series of books on adolescents' health issues provides teens, their parents, their teachers, and all those who work with them accurate information and the tools to keep them safe and healthy. The topics include information about:

- normal growth
- social pressures
- emotional issues
- specific diseases to which adolescents are prone
- stressors facing youth today
- sexuality

The series is a dynamic set of books, which can be shared by youth and the adults who care for them. By providing this information to educate in these areas, these books will help build a foundation for readers so they can begin to work on improving the health and well-being of youth today.

1

Your Teeth:

Why They Are
Important and How
They Developed

The subject of dental care may not seem very exciting . . . at first. After all, how interesting can teeth be? Everybody has them. They don't really appear to do that much. They just sit in your mouth and help you eat. Big deal.

But let's take a closer look.

Your teeth may seem like very passive objects that only become important when you want to chew food, but your teeth actually do much more than that. For example, think for a moment about how pleasurable eating can be. Eating is filled with wonderful sensations. Tasting and feeling the textures of good food brings most people large amounts of pleasure. You probably associate these pleasurable sensations with your tongue and its taste buds, but how good would food taste, how pleasurable would it be, if you had to swallow it whole? Chewing is important because it is one of the first stages of the digestive process, allowing your food to be broken down into smaller particles that will be easy for your stomach to process further. But chewing also releases the flavors and textures in food and plays an active role in your eating experience.

Eating, a process that the average North American engages in at least three times each day, is important to your health and happiness, but it's not the only important process of which your teeth are a part. Throughout each day, your teeth play an active role, not only in your physical health, but in your communication with other people as well. Can you remember when you were a child and lost your teeth? Do you remember how difficult it was to speak with your two front teeth missing? The "s," "th," and "f" sounds just wouldn't come out right. And whistling was impossible! If you've ever had braces, a retainer, worn a mouth guard while playing sports, or lost teeth, you know how big a role your teeth have in speaking. In the English language and in other languages, teeth play an integral part in the production of many sounds. Every time you speak with someone, your teeth are doing an important job.

12

Your Teeth

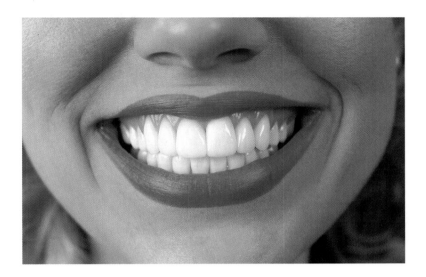

Your mouth plays a vital role in communicating your feelings to the world.

   Communication, however, isn't just about talking. Human beings communicate in many ways. Another form of communication is through facial expressions, and your teeth play an important part in these as well. Through your facial expressions, you can tell people if you're happy or sad, worried or relaxed, thinking or day-dreaming. Your teeth are part of the foundation for the shape of your mouth, and any facial expression involving your mouth also involves your teeth.
   Your smile is the most obvious facial expression in-volving your teeth. Smiling tells other people that you are feeling good, happy, friendly, and open. A smile is a lot like a greeting card. It invites people to join in interac-tion. When you smile, other people feel comfortable around you and you feel good about yourself. A person's

teeth and smile often have a big effect on a person's self-esteem. If you like the way your teeth look, you probably don't hesitate to smile a lot. Smiling and liking your smile make you feel good about yourself. People, however, who don't like the way their teeth look often try to hide their smiles. Feeling unable to smile can make you feel worse about yourself and can hinder social interaction.

So as you can see, your teeth are important, not just for chewing, but for enjoying your food, talking, communicating with others, and for how you feel about yourself. But what are teeth really?

Some animals have many sets of teeth. Sharks, for example, lose their sharp, pointy teeth all the time, but they have seven rows of developing teeth to replace the lost ones. Some sharks have more than 24,000 teeth over a lifetime. But your adult set of teeth is the only set you have! If you lose them, you can never get them back.

Human beings have two sets of teeth. The first is a set of twenty primary teeth. These are often called your "baby" or "milk" teeth. These teeth began to emerge from your *gingiva*, more commonly known as your gums, when you were approximately six months of age. By the time a person is twelve years old, however, the permanent, or adult, set of teeth have replaced most of the primary teeth. This permanent set is composed of thirty-two teeth that you will keep (hopefully) for the rest of your life. Making up this set, known as collective dentition, are four different types of teeth. The incisors, or front teeth, have a thin, jagged edge for biting off food and are the most important teeth for the production of sound. The cuspids (also called the

14

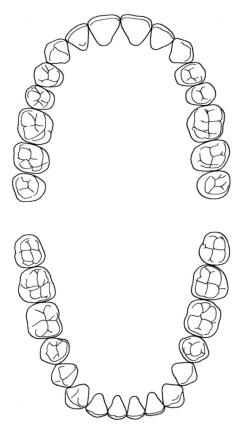

Most adults have thirty-two teeth.

canines) have a long, sharp point for tearing food, while the bicuspids have two points for tearing and crushing. The cuspids and bicuspids also help to shield your other teeth from the damage that comes with daily use. The final category of teeth is the molars, which are squarish and flat for grinding food.

The top, or visible portion of your tooth, is called the crown. The part of your tooth that you cannot see is the long root that anchors your tooth into your jawbone. The

15

outer layer of the root is covered with a hard material called cementum. The remainder of each tooth is composed of three layers. The innermost layer is called the pulp. This is a layer made up mostly of blood vessels and nerves. Vitamin- and mineral-rich blood flow into the pulp to nourish the rest of your tooth. A layer of harder substance, called dentine, encloses the pulp. Dentine is very similar to bone and is the structural component of

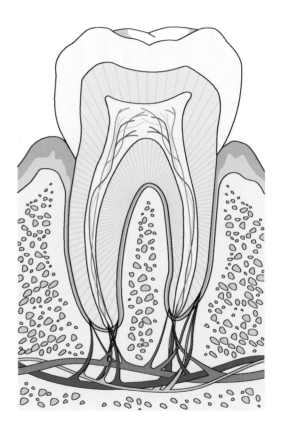

Inside a tooth's enamel is the dentine. The interior of the tooth, the pulp, is fed by blood vessels.

your tooth. Though relatively hard, it is also sensitive and porous with thousands of tubules running through it. The majority of a tooth is composed of dentine. Because the dentine is sensitive and susceptible to damage, it is encased in a final layer called the enamel. Dentine and enamel are both made of up the mineral compounds hydroxyapatite and carbonated hydroxyapatite. The main minerals in these compounds are calcium and phosphate. The protective enamel is the hardest substance in your body. It prevents the foods you eat from coming into contact with and damaging the more delicate parts of your teeth. If you were to think of a tree, the dentine is like the wood of the tree—hard, but relatively easy to damage—and the enamel is like the bark protecting the tree's wood.

The teeth that you have today have been years in the making. Many things affected their development and continue to influence your teeth in the present. You have control over some of these influences, like keeping your teeth clean and eating right, but other conditions of your teeth's development were predetermined and completely out of your control.

The Role of Genetics

Have you ever been told that you have your father's eyes or your mother's smile? Well, in a way, this is very true. As you may know, much of how a person's body develops is determined before that person is even born. This happens when the information, known as **DNA**, housed in the mother's egg and the father's sperm join together to form a completely new set of **chromosomes**. Your forty-six chromosomes are made up of ***genes*** that contain the information for all your physical characteristics like how tall you will be, what color hair you will have, whether you will be susceptible to certain illnesses, and how and when your teeth will develop. The information contained in your DNA will also determine the specific size and shape of your teeth. Some scientists think that how resistant your teeth and gums are to decay and disease may be related to your DNA as well.

Just because your DNA predetermines how and when your teeth should develop doesn't mean that everything will always proceed as your DNA planned. There are many things that can interrupt or alter the course that

Proper dental care can help create a lifetime of healthy teeth, no matter what your genetic history may be.

18

your DNA sets for your teeth. Consider the following example:

Jolleen was five years old when she lost her two front teeth. Unaccustomed to the empty space left in her mouth, Jolleen began to press on her exposed gums with her tongue. Before long, she pressed her tongue into the gap out of habit, hardly even noticing that she was doing it. Jolleen's parents, however, noticed this new habit, but thought it was probably harmless and would soon end once Jolleen's permanent teeth came in. But as the new teeth appeared, Jolleen found she had something else to explore with her tongue. She ran her tongue along the sharp edges beginning to break through her gums. Then, as the teeth emerged, she pressed on the backs of them hard with her tongue. Jolleen's parents were soon alarmed to see that their daughter's teeth were coming in thrust forward with large gaps in between. When they took Jolleen to see the dentist, they were told that her habit was to blame. As she pushed on her teeth day after day, she was slowly forcing the soft, developing teeth into a new position.

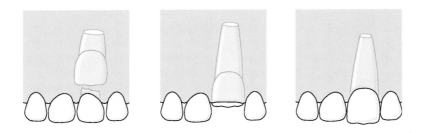

Adult teeth develop inside the gum and push the baby teeth out.

19

Taking Care of Your Smile

In Jolleen's story, we can see how an outside influence changed the path that her DNA had set for her teeth. Situations like Jolleen's are quite common. Losing one's baby teeth is a new and often strange sensation, and it is normal for children to play with loose teeth and gaps in their teeth with their tongues. However, too much of this type of activity can affect how the permanent set of teeth will come in.

Another way that children often alter the position of their teeth is by sucking on their thumbs or fingers. Again, thumb and finger sucking is a very common habit among young children, but if it continues too long, it can have a great effect on the placement of developing teeth. Likewise, children who continue sucking on bottles and pacifiers after their teeth have developed are at risk, not only of changing the position of their teeth, but also of rot in the front teeth, which come in contact with the bottle.

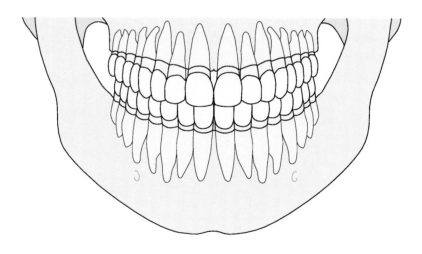

Human beings have both sharp and flat teeth.

20

Physical interventions, like pressing on your teeth with your tongue or sucking on objects, can alter the development *trajectory* of your teeth, but there are many other factors that can influence this development as well. Scientists now know that many of the chemicals and heavy metals released into the environment by industry and waste can alter plant, animal, and human DNA. Radiation can also alter genetic information. A substance capable of altering DNA is called a mutagen. If a person's genetic material were exposed to a mutagen very early in development, and if that mutagen altered the portion of DNA responsible for tooth development, then that person's teeth would develop differently from the original genetic pattern.

You need not be exposed to something as serious as a mutagen, however, to stray from your genetic path. Your DNA is a guide for your *potential* development. In this way, your genetic code is like a recipe for the adult you, but you must remain healthy and have all of the proper "ingredients" for development in order to reach the recipe's full po-

Humans have four different types of teeth, but many animals have only one or two types. Tooth shape is determined by the diets different animals have. Dogs and other carnivores (meat eaters) have large canines and sharp teeth for tearing meat. Cows, horses, and other herbivores (plant eaters) have large, flat teeth for grinding up plants. Human beings need both sharp and flat teeth because we, for the most part, are omnivores, eating both meat and plants.

21

Your genetic code and nutrition are physical factors influencing the development and health of your teeth. However, whether you live in a place where you have access to nutritious food, whether your parents or guardians received education about proper nutrition for their children, and whether your parents or guardians have enough money to afford nutritious food are called socioeconomic factors influencing your development.

tential. Think for a moment about a cake. You can have the best cake recipe in the world, but what happens if you don't have all of the ingredients your recipe calls for? Maybe you substitute some oil for eggs and water for milk. Maybe your oven is broken and you have to bake the cake at 325 degrees instead of 350 degrees. In the end, you might have something that is similar to what your recipe had the potential to produce, but it won't be exactly what the recipe should have produced. If your DNA is a recipe for your development, then the ingredients would be things like air, water, and nutrients.

The Role of Prenatal and Early Childhood Nutrition

The nutrients, or lack of nutrients, you receive in early childhood can have a lifetime effect on your teeth. The **prenatal** period until the age of six are the most important years for the development of a person's body, including his teeth. The foods your mother ate while she was pregnant with you and the foods you ate as a young child determined a lot about the strength and characteristics of your teeth today. Calcium is one of the major ingredients in your teeth, and having enough calcium when you were young and your teeth were developing was necessary for your teeth to be strong and healthy today. Other vitamins and minerals were also important. A lack of proper nutrients when a person is a child can lead to tooth problems later in life.

An example of the importance of prenatal and early childhood nutrition to the later health of your teeth can be seen in people who were born or were children during World War II. In these war years, food in many parts of Europe was very scarce. People had to live on **rations**, and fresh fruits, vegetables, and calcium-rich foods were difficult, often impossible, to find and afford. The people who were children during that war are adults today, and many of them have problems with their teeth like weakness in or loss of enamel, or even **premature** loss of teeth. This is not because people don't take care of their teeth, but because when they were children their teeth didn't have the nutrients necessary to get strong enough to stay healthy for a lifetime.

Of course, this situation is not limited to people who lived in Europe during World War II. All over the world, people living in areas affected by wars, famine, and poverty have a difficult time obtaining or affording nutritious foods. A child in these circumstances, even if she grows up to be a wealthy or privileged adult, would likely have tooth problems in adulthood. Even in North America, a place known throughout the world for its wealth and access to good food, calcium-rich dairy products can be very expensive and difficult for some people to afford. Good prenatal and early-childhood nutrition is a concern in North America as well, and programs like Head

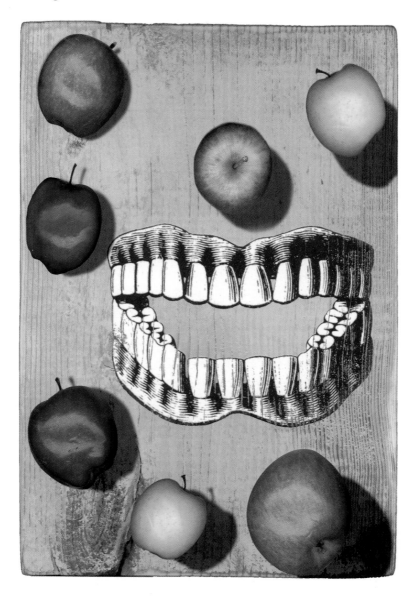

Good nutrtition helps build healthy teeth.

Start, school-lunch programs, Canada Prenatal Nutrition Program and others attempt to provide mothers and children in need with the education and nutrition necessary for developing healthy bodies and minds. Programs for new mothers often encourage breastfeeding (a good way to ensure that a child will get the calcium, vitamins, and other nutrients necessary to grow strong bones and teeth). Other nutrition programs focus on giving children well-rounded diets consisting of a variety of vegetables, fruits, protein, and calcium-rich foods.

Proper nutrition, however, isn't only important when you are a young child. If you are under twenty-one years old, there is a very good chance that at least some of your teeth are still developing. Your final sets of molars usually don't appear until between the ages of eleven and thirteen for your second molars and seventeen and twenty-one for your wisdom teeth. Not everyone gets wisdom teeth, and many people's teeth stop actively developing much earlier, but nevertheless, a healthy, calcium-rich diet remains important for the continued health and strength of your teeth.

2

Take a Bite Out of Decay

Your teeth develop beneath your gum line, but the minute your teeth break through the surface, they are subject to all kinds of potentially damaging influences. The enamel that coats your teeth protects them from many of these dangers, but the sugars in the foods you eat, the hard textures of some foods, and the ever-present bacteria in your mouth, all work together to weaken this enamel and threaten the strength of your teeth. To maintain strong teeth, you must remain ever vigilant in your oral hygiene efforts.

Most tooth problems begin with damage to your tooth enamel. Any weakness in your teeth's enamel is a place where decay can take hold. Plaque is the number one cause of decay you must protect your enamel against. Bacteria are the cause of plaque. Your mouth is always dark and wet, making it the perfect place for bacteria to live. Every moment of every day, bacteria are breeding and multiplying in your mouth and on your teeth. In just a number of hours, there are enough bacteria to form a

Brushing your teeth fights the bacteria that causes cavities.

sticky, clear film on your teeth called plaque. The more hours that go by without brushing, the thicker this film gets.

The two types of bacteria that can cause **caries** or **cavities** in your teeth are streptococci and lactobacilli. These bacteria feed on the sugars in your food. When the bacteria eat these sugars, they give off an acid that can dissolve the enamel on your teeth in a process called demineralization. Just a few minutes after you eat something containing sugar, the bacteria begin this acid production. Luckily, your saliva **neutralizes** and washes away most of the acid. Most acid attacks last for about twenty minutes before your saliva can neutralize them. A serious problem occurs, however, when you have a plaque build-up. The plaque holds the acid next to your teeth, and it is more difficult for your saliva to penetrate sticky plaque. The older and thicker the plaque is, the more difficult it is for your saliva to penetrate and the longer the acid has to attack and dissolve your enamel. After just a few attacks, a weak area can form where even more bacteria, plaque, and sugar can collect to dissolve away more of your tooth. In just a few months, a very serious cavity can result.

Brushing: Your First Line of Defense

Frequent brushing with toothpaste is your first line of defense against bacteria, plaque, and the cavities they cause. Brushing scrapes the bacteria and plaque off of your teeth's surfaces. For brushing to be effective, you must make sure you brush all the surfaces of your teeth—

Taking Care of Your Smile

If you have deep grooves or fissures in your teeth, your dentist may recommend coating your teeth with a sealant to keep food, bacteria, and plaque out of these trouble spots.

the fronts, the backs, and the gum line, and that you brush for at least two minutes. You should use a soft toothbrush so as not to damage your delicate gums. According to the American Dental Association, you should place the toothbrush at a 45-degree angle to your

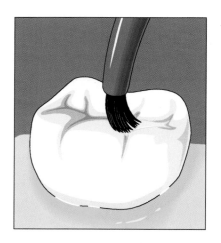

Sealants fill in the tiny cracks in teeth where food and bacteria may collect.

teeth, use small, circular motions on the sides of the teeth, and brush back and forth on the biting or chewing surfaces. Always avoid up-and-down motions. Ideally, you should brush your teeth after every meal. However, in our busy lives, this is not always possible. At the very least, to prevent decay you need to brush two times a day. In addition, you should also always remember to brush your tongue. Bacteria live on your tongue as well as your teeth, and as soon as you close your mouth, bacteria you left on your tongue will migrate right back to your teeth.

If you are like many people, you keep using your toothbrush long after it should be used. Through use, the toothbrush's bristles begin to break down becoming less and less effective over time. After a while, your toothbrush also begins to harbor germs and bacteria, something you definitely don't want more of in your mouth! A toothbrush should be replaced every three to four months. In addition, it's

Did you know that your mouth can support billions of bacteria? There could be more bacteria in your mouth than there are human beings on the face of the earth.

31

also a good idea to change your toothbrush after you've had a cold, flu, or sores in your mouth so that you don't continue to spread those germs around.

When you go into a store to buy a toothbrush, you are confronted with row upon row of tooth-care products, each one claiming to be the best for the health of your teeth. How on earth are you to choose? The truth is, if you are a conscientious brusher who makes sure to brush for at least two minutes and cover all tooth surfaces, then your average, soft-bristle toothbrush, should be adequate. However, many toothbrushes have special designs that can help improve the effectiveness of your brushing. Toothbrushes with flexible handles, diamond-shaped heads, and varied bristle heights can all increase the ease at which you are able to remove plaque from your teeth.

In addition, some people prefer electric toothbrushes, and studies have shown that such toothbrushes, with their small, quickly rotating heads, do remove more plaque than manual brushes. However, when shopping for a toothbrush, you will notice that specialized tooth-brushes are more expensive than simple toothbrushes. If expense is a concern for you, you may want to stick with the simple toothbrush and remember to brush longer and more carefully. If you are worried that your tooth-brush isn't doing its job, or if you find it difficult to reach all the surfaces of your teeth, you should discuss with your dentist what would be the best toothbrush for you.

Your toothpaste also plays an important role in how healthy your teeth are. Toothpaste doesn't actually kill the bacteria in your mouth, but it is *abrasive*, so it helps pull the bacteria off. In this respect, most toothpastes are the same. However, many toothpastes have an important ingredient for your teeth. This ingredient is fluoride. When choosing a toothpaste, you should look for the American Dental Association's or Canadian Dental Asso-ciation's (CDA) seal. This means that these organizations have recognized the toothpaste as containing a *thera-peutic* amount of fluoride.

Fluoride: For a Lifetime of Healthy Teeth

In recent decades, fluoride has led to improved dental health in many countries around the world. Fluoride is a naturally occurring mineral that comes from the element fluorine. Fluoride is found in low levels in water. Sci-entists discovered that small amounts of fluoride

33

strengthen developing teeth and actually help to rebuild tooth material that has been damaged by acid from bacteria. This rebuilding process is called remineralization.

As we already discussed, most of your tooth is made out of the mineral compounds hydroxyapatite and carbonated hydroxyapatite. When fluoride is present, however, it bonds with the other minerals in your teeth, forming a mineral compound called fluorapatite. The resulting tooth material is actually chemically different and more resistant to demineralization from acid.

Because it is so helpful for preventing tooth decay, many communities add fluoride to their water supply in a process called fluoridation. The American Dental Association suggests that water be fluoridated if it has less

Fluoride changes the chemical composition of the tooth surface, making it more resistant to tooth decay.

34

than .7 parts per million (ppm) fluoride. The recommended amount of fluoride is between .7 and 1.2 ppm.

Do you think you consistently brush your teeth for two minutes every time you brush? Very few people actually do, but brushing for at least two minutes is necessary to remove enough plaque to prevent cavities. The next time you brush you teeth, try bringing a stopwatch with you. Begin the watch as you start brushing. Brush for your normal length of time, and stop the watch when you're done. How do you compare to the two-minute requirement?

Measuring something in parts per million can be difficult to visualize. Having water that is one part per million fluoride means that if you divide the water into one million parts, only one of those parts will be fluoride and the other 999, 999 parts will be water or something else. There are one million milligrams in a liter of water. One milligram of fluoride in one liter of water equals one part per million. If you are not familiar with the metric system, it might be easier for you to think of this in another way. Think about the size of a drop that comes out of an eyedropper. One million of these drops fills approximately twenty-five soft-drink bottles. If these bottles contain one part per million fluoride, then out of your twenty-five soft-drink bottles, only one drop is fluoride.

One part per million may seem like a tiny amount of flouride, but it makes a huge difference to your teeth. Studies have shown that water supplies with between .7 and 1.2 ppm fluoride reduce the incidence of cavities in children by up to sixty percent and reduce the incidence of cavities in adults by up to thirty-five percent.

Not everyone in the world can afford dental care or even items like toothbrushes and toothpaste that can improve their dental health. But when a community fluoridates its water supply, everyone in that community benefits with stronger, healthier teeth, regardless of their ability to pay for dental care.

It may seem surprising, but the incidence of tooth loss and decay is actually higher in countries with high standards of living (like the United States, Canada, and England for example) than in countries with a lower standard of living. This is probably due to the fact that people in places like North America and Western Europe have more money to spend on packaged foods, snacks, desserts, and other foods with high sugar contents.

Fluoride, however, isn't always a good thing. Very small quantities of fluoride (what is known as trace amounts) strengthen teeth, but too much fluoride can harm your teeth and your bones. On average, children between the ages of six months and three years should have about .25 milligrams of fluoride per day. Children ages three to six should have about .5 milligrams of fluoride per day, and young people age six to sixteen should have about one milligram of fluoride per day. Ingesting more than the recommended amount of fluoride puts people at risk for developing dental fluorosis, a condition that causes chalky, white spots and streaks in the teeth. Young people whose teeth are still forming are at the greatest risk for developing dental fluorosis from ingesting too much

Healthy white teeth make your smile shine.

fluoride. The risk of dental fluorosis is the main reason children should spit toothpaste out instead of swallowing it.

Even if your community's water supply is not fluoridated, chances are you are still getting fluoride from other sources. Packaged foods that contain water often contain fluoridated water, and many mouthwashes and toothpastes have fluoride as well. Furthermore, in dental visits, it is common for dentists to strengthen your teeth with a treatment of fluoride gel. Fluoride that you ingest in water and food is called *systemic* fluoride. Fluoride that you put on the surfaces of your teeth with toothpastes, mouthwashes, and gels is called *topical* fluoride. Both are important for the strength of your teeth.

Even if you brush conscientiously for two minutes twice each day and ensure that you have the proper amounts of systemic and topical fluoride, you still aren't doing everything necessary to ensure that your teeth and gums stay healthy and cavity- and disease-free. Despite your best efforts with a toothbrush and with fluoride, there are still parts of your teeth that you are not going to be able to reach. For these you will need dental floss.

Flossing: Always Important, Often Ignored

Despite efforts by schools and dentists to educate people on the importance of flossing, the vast majority of people still do not floss on a regular basis. In reality, however, flossing should be as much a part of your daily routine as brushing is. No matter how well and how often you brush, it is still difficult to remove the plaque between

38

your teeth and beneath your gum line. If your teeth are very close together, it is probably impossible that brushing alone will be able to remove all the plaque. For this reason, brushing your teeth, though extremely important, is not enough to ensure that you won't get cavities.

Many people incorrectly believe that the purpose of flossing is just to remove particles of food that get stuck between your teeth and that you need only floss when you have such a lodged particle. This, of course, is not true. The purpose of flossing is the same as brushing: to remove plaque. In addition to brushing, you must floss to remove the stubborn, invisible plaque that builds up around your gums and between your teeth. When you floss, you should wind a long piece of dental floss around your fingers then slip it gently between your teeth. Curve the floss into a C shape, and rub it back and forth around

the side of each tooth. Next, carefully slide the floss up under your gum line in the space between your tooth and gum. Be careful not to jam the floss into your gums, as this can damage the soft tissues. Maintain the curved C shape as you floss beneath the gums. Each time you switch to a new set of teeth, you should use a clean section of the floss so that you don't transfer plaque and bacteria from one part of your mouth to another. Floss comes in both waxed and unwaxed varieties. Both work well for removing plaque, but the waxed floss tends to slide more easily between your teeth and fray less. If your teeth are tight together, you may wish to floss with the waxed variety.

When you floss for the first time, you may notice that your gums bleed. Bleeding of the gums is a sign of periodontal disease, also called gingivitis. Gingivitis, irritation and infection of the gums, is usually caused by tartar, plaque, and the acid given off by the bacteria in your mouth. Most teenagers and adults experience some mild gingivitis from time to time. A tiny bit of bleeding isn't anything to worry about, and in just a few days of regular flossing you will notice the bleeding getting less as your gums get stronger. However, significant bleeding can mean more advanced gum disease, and your dentist should be consulted. Gum disease that goes untreated can eventually infect your tooth sockets and cause tooth loss. You should also be careful as you brush and floss, because even though brushing and flossing are the best ways to prevent gingivitis, if you brush or floss too hard, you can actually irritate your gums and cause gingivitis.

As you now know, plaque builds up in the places that are difficult for your toothbrush to reach, specifically around the gum line and between your teeth. This is where most cavities form. Eventually, if the plaque is not removed, it becomes hard and forms a substance called

Flossing keeps plaque from building up in the tiny cracks between teeth where your toothbrush can't reach.

calculus, more commonly known as tartar. Tartar holds bacteria even more firmly to your teeth. The tartar and bacteria also irritate and damage your soft gum tissue. Plaque is soft enough that you can remove most of it by yourself, but once it becomes tartar, you will probably need to see a dentist to have it removed.

BAD BREATH

Most people aren't only concerned about the health and look of their teeth, but also the smell of their breath. And with good reason! Bad breath can be a real *inhibitor* to social interaction. Have you ever experienced the anxiety of going through a day worrying about your breath smelling bad? When you're worried about how your breath smells, it can be hard to smile and talk naturally with other people. You may find yourself hiding your mouth behind your hands, trying to maintain distance between yourself and others, and keeping your mouth tight-lipped. To make matters worse, you may not be able to tell whether you have bad breath or not. Usually it is easier for other people to smell your breath than for you to smell your own.

The technical term for bad breath is halitosis. As embarrassing as it can be to have bad breath, the reality is that we all experience halitosis sometimes. But, like plaque, bad breath is usually easy to keep under control with brushing and flossing. Decomposing food trapped between teeth and under gums is one of the major causes of bad breath. If you have never flossed before, or if it has been a long time since you last flossed, you might notice an unpleasant odor when you slip the floss between your teeth and beneath your gums. This is usually because small particles of food stuck in these areas begin to rot. If you floss daily, you will no longer notice a smell because the food particles will be removed before they have time to decompose.

Another trouble spot for halitosis is your tongue. People often forget to brush their tongue, and thus not only transfer bacteria back to their newly brushed teeth, but leave bacteria behind to cause bad breath. When you brush, always remember to brush your tongue thoroughly with long, back to front strokes.

Many people rely on breath mints, sprays, gum, and mouthwash to deal with their bad breath. These items can cover up bad breath for a little while, but they soon wear off. Brushing and flossing actually remove the bacteria and the decomposing food that are causing the bad breath. Antiseptic mouthwashes have also been shown to kill the bacteria in your mouth, but they should only be used in addition to brushing and flossing, never as a substitute! Furthermore, most mouthwash is not antiseptic and will only cover up smells, not eliminate them. Make sure to read the label and look for the American Dental Association's or Canadian Dental Association's seal when choosing a mouthwash for bad breath.

In addition to the typical food particles and bacteria that cause bad breath, there can be other causes as well. A lack of saliva in the mouth will cause bad breath. Anything that reduces saliva, such as breathing through your mouth, not drinking enough fluids, not eating regularly, smoking, certain health conditions, and some medications, can have a negative impact on your breath. Drinking fluids, especially water, frequently throughout the day can help keep your mouth moist and your breath fresh. An excessively dry mouth can be a sign of other

Dental care can be expensive, so people sometimes put off seeing their dentist. However, regular dental visits are important to keeping your teeth healthy.

medical conditions, so if you find your mouth is dry all of the time, you should consult your dentist or doctor.

Bad breath can also result from the foods you eat, such as onions and garlic, or from nasal or sinus infections. If you are brushing multiple times each day, flossing, using antiseptic mouthwash, drinking enough fluids, and eating properly and you still can't control your bad breath, you should speak to your dentist or doctor. They have treatments that can help.

Now you know some of the most basic elements of good oral hygiene, but you're not done yet. Even if you follow all of these guidelines, there's still something else you need to do. As long as your teeth remain healthy, you should visit the dentist for a professional cleaning and check up twice each year. Many people think that if their teeth seem fine they can skip these routine check ups and cleanings, but routine visits to the dentist can identify potential weaknesses in your teeth before they become problems like cavities and decay. Preventing tooth problems is much less troublesome, costly, and painful than fixing them later on. Nevertheless, most people eventually experience at least one tooth problem, such as a cavity or an injury, that only a dentist can fix. Luckily, today's dentists have access to vast amounts of information and technology and can fix dental problems in amazing ways.

If you are like many people, you may get nervous, even fearful, at the thought of going to the dentist. It is true that even as little as a few decades ago a visit to the dentist could mean a great deal of discomfort. Huge strides have been made in dentistry, and though we may never count going to the dentist among our favorite activities, there is no longer reason for young people to fear the dentist's chair. However, a quick look into the past can show us why so many people grew to fear the dentist and why some people refer to today as the age of painless dentistry.

3

THE HISTORY OF DENTISTRY

When you look through the doorway into a dentist's office today, you are glimpsing some of our society's most advanced technology. Dentistry is a highly skilled field of knowledge involving everything from pain management to precise surgical procedures. Most people know that it requires years of training and education to become a dentist. What you may not know is that when a person finally graduates from these many years of schooling, she enters into a medical tradition that has existed for thousands of years.

Long before our modern-day dentists emerged, long before medicine even had specialized fields like dentistry, human beings were forced to find ways to deal with the problems their teeth would cause. Prehistoric human beings had very poor diets. Their food was hard and tough. The skulls of these prehistoric people show us that their teeth were very worn down from this food. Poor diet and poor oral hygiene resulted in other problems as well. Today, living with so much modern technology, a toothache or an infection in your mouth probably doesn't seem very serious, but at that time, if a decaying tooth caused a serious gum infection, for example, a person could die without proper treatment. In those days, how-

The ancient Egyptians may have been the first people to drill their teeth to treat infections.

48

ever, people certainly didn't have things like toothpaste and antiseptic mouthwash, so what was "proper" treatment for problems of teeth?

An ancient piece of writing from 5000 B.C.E. shows us that the Sumerians, a civilization that lived in the area that is present-day Iraq, believed that toothaches and decay were caused by "tooth worms." In China, and later in Western society, people also believed in tooth worms. It wasn't until the eighteenth century that the belief in tooth worms was challenged by more modern forms of science.

The Ancient Egyptians were some of the first people to develop specialized dental care techniques. Ancient Egypt was a civilization that existed over 5,000 years ago and lasted for thousands of years. The civilization is quite well known today, partly because much of the society's writing, known as hieroglyphs, has survived in the dry desert climate of Egypt on a type of paper known as papyrus. The Egyptian's embalming techniques, in which human bodies were *mummified*, allow us to closely examine their teeth and learn about what dentistry may have looked like in this ancient civilization.

What do mummies tell us about Egyptian teeth? Mummies speak silently to us and share the secrets of ancient Egypt. Like those of their prehistoric ancestors, Egyptians' teeth were hurt by neglect and the coarse diet they ate. The teeth of mummies are well worn, probably from the way that the Egyptians milled their grain. They used rough stones to grind the grain into a coarse meal, but in the process, parts of the stone would be ground into the grain as well. To make matters worse, Egypt has very sandy soil and the sand probably got into the food and was accidentally consumed. In Egypt, it did not matter whether a person was rich or poor. The problem of coarse food affected everyone. Even the teeth of Pharaohs are worn and look neglected.

Mummies also reveal how severe tooth rot and decay affected the ancient Egyptians. Some of the problems must have been very painful. Sometimes tooth infections were so severe that they spread to jawbones.

Medical practitioners specializing in different sorts of illnesses can be found in Egyptian history at least as long ago as the time period referred to as the Old Kingdom, which dates from about 3100 to 2100 B.C.E. Some of these experts treated only dental ailments. In fact, the first dental specialist that we know about, a person by the name of Hesi-Re, came from Egypt. Hesi-Re died around 2600 B.C.E. He was described in an inscription on his tomb as "the greatest of the physicians who dealt with the teeth." Early specialists like Hesi-Re began to introduce new ideas into dental treatment.

Adding to the many mysteries shrouding the Egyptians are discoveries that show Egyptians must have had a working drill of some kind. Perfectly symmetrical drill holes in the jaws of mummies have been found. It could have been that the drill holes were meant to relieve the pressure caused by things like infection. If someone had a painful build-up of puss in the gum, she might have had her jawbone drilled. This may seem brutal today, but at that time the drill was extremely advanced technology.

Whereas mummies show us that drilling into gums and jawbones was done, probably to relieve pressure and ease pain, they also show us that the teeth themselves were not operated on. When a person was afflicted with a less serious dental problem, instead of drilling into a

Our modern dental instruments are probably not very different from the instruments ancient people used to pull teeth.

51

The ancient Greeks' influence can still be seen today in our own art, philosophy, and medicine.

person's bone, Egyptian medical prac-titioners used herbal (or plant-based) remedies. Furthermore, in Egypt, religious priests often served as the medical practitioners, and ideas about caring for the body and healing illness were connected to ideas of spirituality and the gods. Many of the problems that the Egyptians faced could have been avoided by the simple things we do today, like brushing. To the Egyptians, however, it seems oral hygiene was not much of a concern.

Today Hippocrates is best known as the creator of the Hippocratic Oath. The Hippocratic Oath is a promise which most medical students give to "do no harm." The versions that still exist today vary from school to school and are different than the oath first given by Hippocrates. Medical students today, for example, do not swear against the use of the knife in practicing medicine. Could you imagine a surgeon swearing never to use a knife?

It was not until the age of ancient Greece that beginnings of modern medicine and tooth extraction as we recognize them today began to emerge. By about the sixth century B.C.E., the Greek world was firmly established, and its influence on philosophy, medicine, and language is still felt today. For example, many of our English words come from Greek. Did you know that the root word of orthodontist is based on the Greek word *odous* for tooth? An orthodontist is someone who treats the irregular alignment of teeth.

The founder of modern medicine was Hippocrates, who lived from around 460 B.C.E. to about 377 B.C.E. He practiced and taught at many of the medical schools of Greece, including in the cities of Athens and Cos. He

53

started looking at medicine **rationally** and scientifically. This differed from the religious-based view of medicine that was traditionally practiced in Egypt and elsewhere around the world.

The ancient Greeks valued their teeth, and a full, healthy set was prized. When a tooth had to be extracted, the tool used was a simple pair of dental *forceps*, known as *odontagra*. This instrument was very similar to a set of pliers and required little skill to use. Hippocrates said that the only time a tooth should be extracted was when it was loose. If you can imagine having your teeth pulled out by someone using only a set of pliers, you might be able to see why Hippocrates made his recommendation.

Around the time when Hippocrates died, one of the most influential philosophers to ever live was born. His name was Aristotle and he lived from 384 to 322 B.C.E.

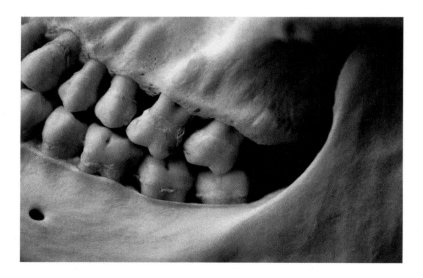

Researchers can learn about past cultures' dental care by studying the teeth and skulls of the people who lived in those times.

Aristotle, like Hippocrates, wrote about dentistry, including the treatment of decayed teeth and extracting teeth with forceps. One difference between the two thinkers is that Aristotle did not limit the use of the *odontagra* to only loose teeth, but thought that it could be used to remove teeth still firmly rooted if it was necessary.

Despite the high value the Greeks placed on their teeth, it was not until Greece was taken over by Rome and became a province of the Roman Empire that the Greeks began to take a greater measure of care in preventing decay.

Rome rose as a world power with a sprawling empire surrounding the Mediterranean Sea, including in its boundaries much of Europe and a great deal of the Middle East. It treated Greek knowledge of philosophy, religion, and science with a special reverence. At Roman civilization's height, from around 146 B.C.E. to about A.D. 476, Rome built on Greek thought and made great strides in many scientific and technological fields.

While it borrowed from Greek culture, Rome was also built upon an older existing civilization called Etruria. The information we have of this group is scarce. Almost all of it comes from examining Etruscan tombs, which were faithfully designed as copies of Etruscan homes. Etruscan artifacts, including dentures made out of bands of gold that held replacement teeth, have been found.

It seems funny to think at first, but plumbing was one of the greatest Roman achievements. A little thinking, however, and you can probably imagine some pretty good reasons why plumbing is such a big technological advance. Roman cities were linked to sources of water by massive aqueducts, large overland architectural structures that transported water great distances. An aqueduct looks like a long bridge, except instead of transporting people, water is channeled over its surface.

55

The toothbrush is a more recent invention than toothpaste.

In the cities, homes were equipped with metal pipes and, as a result, many had running water. At the same time, Rome's extensive empire brought in a great amount of wealth and the best and brightest people residing throughout the Mediterranean region were attracted to the capital. Many Greek physicians and scientists flocked to Rome. Good plumbing meant better hygiene. Better hygiene resulted in more cleanliness and less diseases of the mouth. The knowledge of Greek physicians added to the advancing field of dental care.

In the ancient world, cultures often interacted in peacefulness, learning from each other and improving humankind's well being. While the Romans gained from such learned Greek physicians, like Dioscorides, who served in the army of Emperor Nemo, the Greeks also gained. The Romans introduced to the Greeks various tooth cleaners, including pumice, talc, emery, ground alabaster, coral powder, and iron dust. To us, accustomed to the fresh taste of mint toothpaste morning and night, these things might seem unappetizing, but they were among the first cleansers that people ever used.

In most people's minds, toothbrushes are associated with toothpaste. It might surprise you to learn that toothpaste was actually invented in China thousands of years before the toothbrush.

One example of the interaction between cultures is the journey of the toothbrush. It was invented by the Chinese in 1500 B.C.E. Given that Egyptians had been dealing with dental problems with drills thousands of years before this, it seems to be a very long time for something as simple as a toothbrush to come about. Europeans borrowed the idea of the toothbrush from the Chinese when China and Europe became closer because of more trade ties. At the time, the closest thing that existed in England was a cloth-wrapped stick or finger. Europe's nobility and gentry had been using toothpicks and scrapers for centuries, but the toothbrush took some time to catch on.

In the early Middle Ages in Europe (from about A.D. 500 to 1000), Catholic monks generally performed medical procedures like pulling teeth and performing surgery because they were the most highly educated people in the society. But there was a problem. The monks had the education to perform medicine, but they did not have the tools. However, as you may know, Catholic monks always have their heads shaved. Because of this, barbers were frequent visitors to the monasteries. The barbers who came to the monasteries to shave the monks' heads had tools like sharp knives and razors, so they often served as assistants to the medical procedures. In the twelfth century, however, the Catholic Church passed a number of laws forbidding monks to perform any of these medical procedures. But these laws couldn't stop people from needing surgeries and tooth extractions. The monks, no longer able to perform the procedures themselves, taught the barbers their medical skills. Soon the barber-surgeon, a person who worked as a barber, surgeon, and dentist, was born. The role of the barber-surgeon continued for many centuries both in Europe and later in European-colonized North America.

For centuries, the continents of North and South America had much less recorded contact with the civilizations of Europe and Asia than other parts of the world. Although today we know that Vikings traveled to areas of North America, including Newfoundland, Labrador, and probably Baffin Island in the Canadian Arctic archipelago, most people still associate "discovery" of the New World with Christopher Columbus in 1492.

At the time that Christopher Columbus landed in the Americas, there existed a people known as the Mayans. The Mayans lived in the area that is now Southern Mexico, Guatemala, and Honduras and had an advanced, pyramid-building civilization. In the sixteenth century, Spanish **conquistadors** came to the Americas and set out to claim as much land for the Spanish Crown as possible. Under the guise of spreading Christianity, the Spanish effectively destroyed much of Mayan culture. Many, many Mayans were murdered and eventually the entire civilization was destroyed. Motivated by a religious *fervor* that equated Mayan beliefs and culture with the Christian Devil, the Spanish conquistadors and missionaries also wiped out most of the Mayans' writings. The result is not only that a civilization was destroyed, but

The ancient Mayans' civilization was destroyed by the Spanish conquerors.

59

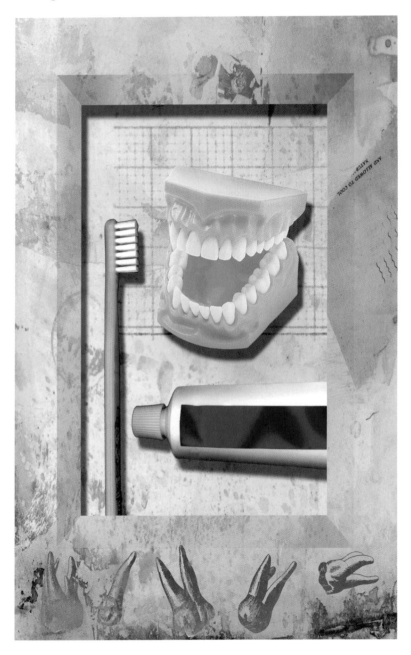

also that a great deal of valuable knowledge has been lost to humanity.

Not much evidence exists showing that the Mayans performed medical dentistry. However, artifacts that remain from their culture do show that the Mayans performed what appears to be *cosmetic* dentistry. Today people have cosmetic dentistry done for a number of reasons. For example, a person might wish to straighten his teeth to construct what our culture considers to be a more perfect smile. Similar cultural values probably motivated many Mayans, but the results were quite different. Instead of braces, Mayans inlaid their teeth with precious and semi-precious stones such as turquoise, onyx, and jade. This must have been a very painful procedure as it was done by drilling a hole into the center of the tooth and inserting the stone. Since we know so little about Mayan culture, we can't be sure what the significance of these stones was, but they were possibly placed for religious, familial, or beauty enhancement purposes.

One thing we do know about Mayan dentistry is that the Mayans were the first to implant false teeth into the living body. Other civilizations had already experimented and had varying levels of success with dentures that were placed on top of the gums or remains of teeth. By implanting material like shells or stones into the body, however, the Mayans went well beyond simple dentures. The procedure of inserting false teeth is known by a technical term called *endosseous alloplastic*. This means that a material is actually ***grafted*** into the bone and takes hold. There is no earlier record of this procedure being done anywhere else. In fact, the modern procedure of endosseous alloplastic did not develop until the twentieth century. In this respect, the Mayans were certainly ahead of their time, and it has taken us centuries to catch up!

61

Taking Care of Your Smile

Since Christopher Columbus's arrival in the Americas, the development of modern dentistry has progressed largely in accordance with science's major discoveries. Great advances were made in Europe during the four-teenth, fifteenth, and sixteenth centuries, the period of time known as the Renaissance. The word Renaissance means rebirth. Throughout much of the Renaissance, Europeans borrowed their ideas from the ancient cul-tures of Greece and Rome as well as other civilizations, like China. By the seventeenth century, however, a new generation of European thinkers was changing the way that people in Europe saw the world. You might have heard of some of them, including Galileo, who hypothe-sized that the Earth revolves around the sun, and New-ton, who theorized about gravity.

During the Renaissance, fields of knowledge from the fine arts to science developed and advanced at an in-credible pace. Dentistry, however, seems to have taken off more slowly in this time period than the general field of medicine. This was because dentistry was not yet a specialized field. At the time, dentistry was not taught in universities. Instead, some people took apprenticeships, while others were self-taught. Guilds of barber-surgeons continued to operate during the Renaissance as they had before it. Many of these guild members traveled through-out the countryside in order to reach people outside of the major cities. Anesthesia was not yet discovered, and the work was often done without any kind of pain con-trol. You can imagine that many people must have been quite nervous to have a tooth removed without painkillers by a traveling, self-taught "surgeon."

Despite the poor state of dentistry at the time, the great thinkers of Europe were learning about things that were soon adopted into the dental field. With the adoption of the microscope, microorganisms and bacteria were discovered. Medical advances and discoveries about the human body also helped to establish better dental knowledge. The invention and increasing use of the printing press helped to spread news of these advances.

Today's modern scientific profession of dentistry is largely the result of the work of a Frenchman, Pierre Fauchard, and a man from Great Britain, John Hunter. Before he died in 1761, Fauchard influenced many other dentists, making dentistry a specialized field. John Hunter made a huge contribution to dentistry by documenting the human mouth, painstakingly creating a book called *The Natural History of the Human Teeth: Explaining Their Structure, Use, Formation, Growth and Diseases*, which was published in 1771.

Shortly after the American Revolution and the founding of the United States of America, many American dentists were still going to Europe to get their training. By the middle of the nineteenth century, however, the scientists and dentists of the United States began to make important contributions to dentistry. Many of these American advances had very practical uses. The discovery of anesthesia occurred in the United States in the 1840s and made extracting teeth and performing necessary dental work much easier for both the patient and the doctor. Ether and nitrous oxide, also known as laughing gas, were the most popular anesthetics. Anesthesia was quickly introduced into both Canada and Europe and heralded a whole new age in medicine and science. In this Modern Period, many people believed that science

> In the eighteenth century in England and the English colonies in North America, the local blacksmith sometimes served as the local dentist.

and rationality could solve the mysteries of nature. They saw anesthetics' triumph over pain as evidence to support their beliefs.

> Did you know that during World War II, one in five of the first two million American recruits were turned away because they did not meet the military's basic dental requirement that they have at least three sets of molars and three sets of incisors? That's just twelve teeth.

Another American pioneering feat in the field of dentistry was the first dental school in the world. It was called The Baltimore College of Dental Surgery and was established in 1840. The need for experts trained in the specialized field had greatly increased. There were a large number of fakes or "quacks" who pretended to know something about dentistry, but actually did not. They often took people's money without providing proper services, and they sometimes caused physical harm to people.

With quacks and fakes posing as dentists, there was a need to organize into a national group to regulate standards of professionalism for dentists. The dental profession in the United States was based along regional lines. This meant that dentists in different states belonged to different organizations. In 1859, a small group of dentists met in Niagara Falls, New York, and decided to join their organizations together. This new organization was called the American Dental Association and today seven out of ten American dentists belong to it.

Like Europe and the United States, Canada's first dentists of European descent were actually barber-surgeons. Their presence dates to around the middle of the seventeenth century in Quebec. Shortly after the American Revolution, Canada experienced a large influx of immigrants from the former English colonies in what had become the United States of America. These people were known as the United Empire Loyalists. Among them were a number of dentists.

Dentists in Canada, like those in the United States, realized the need for a proper organization. The first such organization was the Ontario Dental Association, which was created on July 2, 1867, the day after three of the remaining British colonies in North America confederated. These colonies became the four provinces of Nova Scotia, New Brunswick, Quebec, and Ontario and were united as a single country called Canada. The Ontario

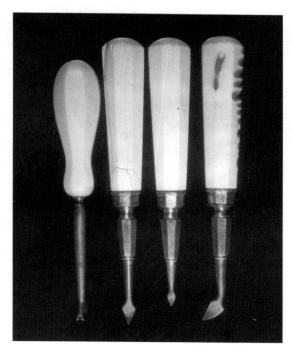

Nineteenth-century dental instruments.

Dental Association was the idea of Barnabus Day, a medical graduate of Queen's University in Kingston, Canada. It was not until 1902, however, that a national organization was established.

Although dentistry historically has been dominated by men, in North America, it did not take women long to enter into the schools. Women's numbers were small at first, but women have been a part of dental education from the beginning. In 1866, Lucy Hobbs Taylor became the first woman in the United States to graduate from a dental school. Emelie Foeking soon followed, graduating

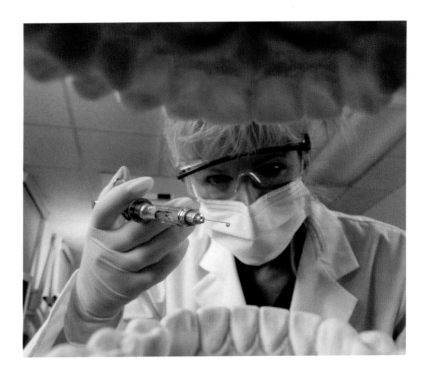

Today, many dentists are women.

from The Baltimore College of Dental Surgery in 1873. Two years after this, in 1875, Canada founded its first degree-granting medical school called The Royal College of Dental Surgeons (R.C.D.S.). The first Canadian woman to ever graduate with a degree in dentistry was C.L. Josephine Wells who earned her degree from the R.C.D.S. in 1893.

In today's world, we are used to rapidly changing education, science, and technology. Technological changes through the last two centuries have happened with increasing speed. We now widely use the electric drill, another American invention which has become commonplace in dentist offices throughout the world. Cutting-edge metal alloys are now used to fill cavities and to crown decayed or destroyed teeth. Dentists have also perfected the use of a German invention, the X-ray machine.

Just like the rising standards of technology, society's standards for dental care rose during the twentieth century. Today, dental offices are no longer places to fear. They are equipped with the best tools, the most effective anesthesia and pain reducers, and some of the most educated professionals. Furthermore, North Americans' dental health as a whole has improved. Over the years, citizens have pushed governments to act to improve the dental health of the public. As a result, most of us now drink from a fluoridated water supply. For the most part, our diets are more varied and nutritious. Some of the most serious problems that ancient Egyptians suffered because of their diet do not affect North Americans. One final important difference is education. We are also now taught from grade school onwards that proper care and prevention goes a lot further toward maintaining healthy teeth and gums than having to be treated for a problem after it develops.

4.

DECAYERS AND STAINERS

A trip to the dentist is no longer the thing to fear that it once was. Nevertheless, you would probably prefer to limit your dental visits to your two yearly cleanings. The healthier your teeth are and the fewer cavities you have, the less serious dental care you will need. Unfortunately, the incidence of cavities actually rises in the teenage years. This rise in cavity rates is most likely caused by the poor dietary choices some teens make. As a teen, you are away from your parents for longer periods of time and have a greater ability to choose the foods that you want to eat. Teenagers also tend to snack more than children or adults. Having more freedom over the foods you eat, being away from home for longer hours, and snacking more frequently often lead to sugar being present in your mouth for longer periods of time.

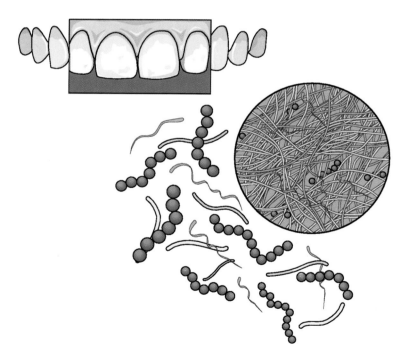

Bacteria feed on the sugar that sticks to your teeth.

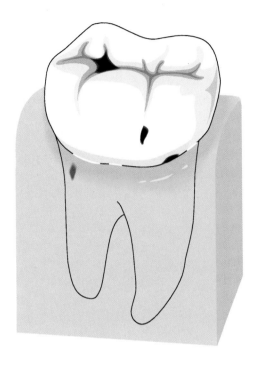

Cavities are caused by tooth decay.

Sugar: Master Decayer #1

As we discussed earlier, having a high concentration of sugar present in your mouth is the greatest cause of tooth damage and decay. One of the most effective ways to reduce your risk of getting cavities is to reduce your sugar intake.

Reducing the amount of sugar you eat can actually be trickier than it seems. Sweet foods like candy and cookies are obviously high in sugar, and it's easy to understand

71

why they might harm your teeth. But sugar comes in many forms, and even foods that are very good for you can weaken your teeth.

All carbohydrates are sugars, but not all sugars are particularly dangerous to your teeth. The sugars you must be most concerned with are the monosaccharides, or the simple sugars. There are five types of monosaccharides: glucose, sucrose, fructose, lactose, and maltose. Glucose is the type of sugar that your body uses for energy, and all other sugars are broken down into glucose by your body. Sucrose is the sugar that you find in candy or in your kitchen's sugar bowl. It comes from sugar cane, sugar beets, or sugar maple trees. Sucrose tastes very sweet to your tongue, and you can easily tell if something you are eating contains sucrose in high quantities.

Fructose is the type of sugar found in fruit, honey, and corn. It is generally not as sweet as sucrose. However, it is often concentrated into something known as corn syrup

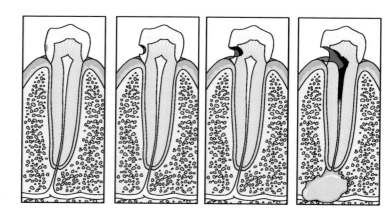

Sometimes, a cavity can become so bad that it causes an abscess at the tooth root. This painful condition is usually treated with a root canal.

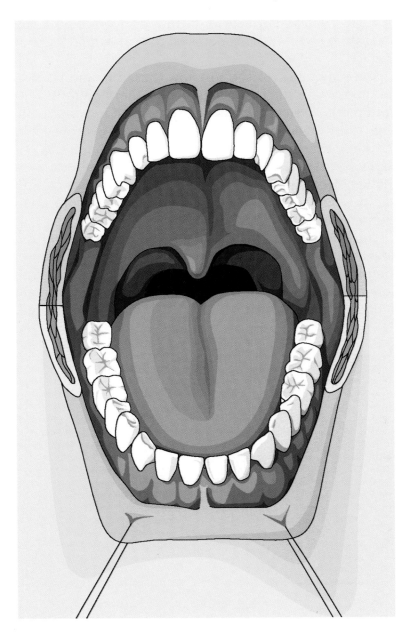

or high-fructose corn syrup. In this concentrated form, fructose is sweeter than sucrose and even worse for your teeth.

You may be surprised to know that milk and cheese, foods that are high in calcium and therefore good for your teeth, also contain a sugar that is bad for your teeth. This is the sugar lactose. Lactose does not taste sweet in the same way that sucrose and fructose do, but it can still harm your teeth. Although you don't want to limit your intake of calcium-rich foods the same way you limit candy, you should rinse your mouth or clean your teeth after eating foods containing lactose.

The final simple sugar that can harm your teeth is the sugar found in grains—the sugar maltose. Like lactose, maltose does not have a candy-sweet taste, and therefore you may not be aware when you are eating it that you are actually eating a form of sugar. Many forms of alcohol,

Brushing your teeth twice a day is an important step toward preventing cavities.

like beer, are brewed from grains and therefore contain the sugar maltose.

For the most part, brushing twice a day and flossing once each day should be enough to prevent cavities. However, it is always a good idea to also brush your teeth after eating something that contains a lot of sugar. This is especially important if you eat lots of sugary foods. Carrying a toothbrush and some toothpaste in your backpack can help you be prepared for the unexpected sugary snack. Of course, we all live busy lives, and it's not always convenient to pull out a toothbrush and start brushing our teeth every time we eat something. If you are in a situation in which you absolutely can't brush your teeth after eating something sugary, you should at least try to swish some water around your mouth. Even this will help to wash the food particles, sugar, and acid away from the surfaces of your teeth. An additional benefit is that periodically swishing your mouth with water can also help to combat bad breath.

Acid: Master Decayer #2

By now you are already well aware that the bacteria in your mouth feed on sugar and give off acid that dissolves the surfaces of your teeth. However, the acid from bacteria is not the only acid that will harm your teeth.

Scientists use something known as the pH scale to determine the level of acidity of a substance. Pure water has a pH of seven and is considered neutral. Anything with a pH lower than seven is acidic, and anything with a pH higher than seven is basic. Any acidic substance will dissolve the minerals of your teeth, and plenty of foods con-

pH level	Substance
1	Battery Acid
2.49	Pepsi
2.53	Coca-Cola
2.82	Hawaiian Fruit Punch
2.95	Gatorade
3	Vinegar
3.04	Nestea
3.22	Mountain Dew
4.61	Barq's Root Beer
5	Rainwater
6	Milk
7	Pure water
8	Egg Whites
9	Baking Soda
10	Antacid Tablets
11	Ammonia
12	Mineral Lime
13	Drano
14	NaOH

tain acid. The more acidic the substance is, the more minerals it will dissolve.

Are you curious about the strength of the acid in the soda you drink? Try this experiment. Take an oxidized penny—one that has turned greenish with age—and drop it into a glass of your favorite soft drink. Let a few minutes go by then check the penny. How much oxidization has dissolved? Drop the penny back in and let it sit for a number of hours. How long does it take for the penny to get shiny and look new again? Now what do you think your soda is doing to your teeth?

Some of the most prevalent acids in food are citric acid and phosphoric acid. Soft drinks are some of the worst foods for triggering acid attacks on your teeth because they contain citric and phosphoric acids as well as sugar. When you drink soft drinks, you are bathing your whole mouth in acid and sugar. The same thing occurs when you drink an alcoholic beverage like beer or wine. These are also high in sugar and are acidic.

Many people think that by drinking sugar-free soft drinks they are eliminating the danger to their teeth, but this is clearly not true. Sugar-free soft drinks still contain acid, and although the bacteria in your mouth aren't getting a snack, your teeth are still being attacked. Like high-sugar foods, it is good to limit your consumption of these carbonated beverages.

The Stainers

Decay is not the only thing you should be concerned about when considering the health of your teeth. Many foods and beverages can stain your teeth, making your teeth look less healthy and making you look older.

Coffee, tea, and red wine are some of the strongest stainers of teeth. Many people consume coffee and tea on a daily basis. These dark drinks have a great ***cumulative*** effect on the color of a person's teeth. Some medications, like certain antibiotics, can cause permanent stains on your teeth. Things like foods and beverages that stain your teeth from the outside are external causes of staining, while things like medication that affect the inside of your tooth are internal causes of staining. Staining also tends to increase with age. Over years of wear, the surfaces of your teeth develop tiny cracks and irregularities. These changes may be invisible to the naked eye, but they make your teeth much more susceptible to stains.

> Canadians drink 40 million cups of coffee each day. There are only 31 million Canadians! Americans drink 350 million cups of coffee each day. There are only 288 million Americans!

One of the worst things you can do for your teeth and your body is smoke. You've probably heard people call smoking a dirty habit. This is quite literally true. When you smoke, you pull millions of tiny, harmful particles into your mouth and lungs. The tar and chemicals in cig-

Smoking stains your teeth and can contribute to tooth decay.

arettes stain your teeth, making your teeth look yellow and dirty. Furthermore, smoking causes terribly bad breath. The smoke and chemicals smell bad on their own, but in addition, smoking reduces the amount of saliva in your mouth. With less saliva to wash away sugar, bacteria, and acid, odor- and decay-causing bacteria multiply. If you are a smoker, one of the best things you can do for your teeth, mouth, and whole body is stop smoking today. Your dentist can give you advice on stopping smoking and restoring your pearly-white smile.

TOOTH-WHITENING PRODUCTS

If you already have stains on your teeth, there are a number of products currently available that can help. You probably see such products advertised all the time on television promising a gleaming, youthful smile, but be aware. Not all tooth-whitening products are safe or effective. Of those that are safe, some work better than others.

Tooth-whitening procedures will not necessarily work on all types of stains. External stains caused by foods and beverages may respond well to whitening procedures, while internal stains or graying from age or poor nutrition will not respond well. Furthermore, only your tooth

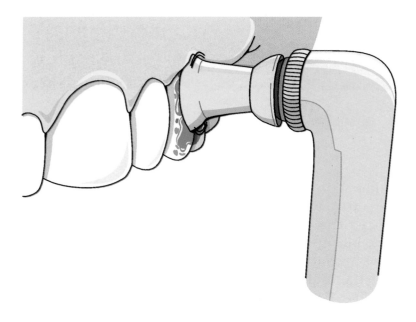

Dentists have special instruments to clean teeth.

material will respond to bleaching. Any tooth-colored fillings or cement on your teeth will not change color. There are three categories of tooth-whitening products you can choose from: in-office bleaching, at-home bleaching, and whitening toothpastes.

If you choose to have in-office bleaching, your dentist will apply a bleaching agent to your teeth. Your dentist may then shine a special light on your teeth. This light stimulates the bleaching agent. While your teeth are undergoing bleaching, your delicate gum tissues will need to be protected by a rubber shield or a special gel. The American Dental Association (ADA) has determined that these in-office bleaching procedures are safe and effective.

Another option for tooth whitening is at-home bleaching. The active bleaching agents in at-home kits are peroxides. You can get at-home bleaching kits from your dentist, or you can buy tooth-bleaching products from a grocery store or pharmacy. These products may be applied to your teeth with trays, strips, or paint-on gels. However, only kits from your dentist containing ten percent carbamide peroxide are recognized by the ADA.

Your other option for tooth whitening is a whitening toothpaste. Toothpastes in general are mildly abrasive, and this abrasiveness helps to lift stains off of the enamel. Whitening toothpastes are generally more abrasive than other toothpastes and can lift stains to a greater degree. As with other tooth-care products, you should look for the ADA or CDA seal of acceptance when choosing a product.

5

CONSTRUCTING THE "PERFECT" SMILE

If you live in North America and are between the ages of ten and fourteen, you probably know a lot of people who have braces. In fact, you may very well have braces yourself. But if you were to look at people of the same age group around the world, you would notice that most of them do not have braces. So why are braces such a phenomenon in North America, and what is it that they do?

BRACES:
WHAT YOU SHOULD KNOW

In North America, millions of people have braces. Braces consist of pieces of metal, plastic, or porcelain adhered to the surfaces of the teeth. Wires are run between these

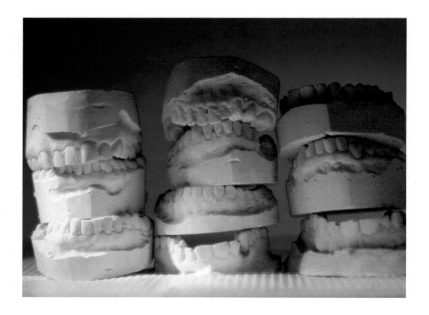

Orthodontists often make casts of individuals' teeth to help them see what treatment needs to occur.

84

pieces and then adjusted to pull and push the teeth into different positions. Braces can be used for different purposes. These purposes can be either cosmetic or medical. In most cases, they are a combination of the two.

North American ideals of the beautiful smile may seem natural to you. You might assume that everyone in the world desires straight, gleemingly white teeth, but this is not the case. Ideas about what is beautiful are culturally relative. For example, for centuries in Japan, Vietnam, and other Asian countries people thought it was beautiful for women to blacken their teeth. A mixture containing iron filings was painted on the teeth to dye them black. This practice continued right up to the nineteenth century.

When braces are used for medical purposes, it is to correct something known as a *malloclusion*. A malloclusion is a problem with a person's bite. In some malloclusions, the lower jaw is too small or set too far back, causing the upper teeth to extend out over the lower teeth in what is called an overbite. Sometimes the opposite is the case, and the upper jaw is too small causing an underbite. In other situations, a person's teeth might be crowded, overlapping, twisted, or otherwise crooked.

A malloclusion can cause serious dental problems. If one's teeth don't line up properly, certain teeth can get worn down more quickly than others or problems can develop in the jawbones. A very serious malloclusion could make chewing properly difficult and inhibit the digestive process. In cases like these, braces can become a

85

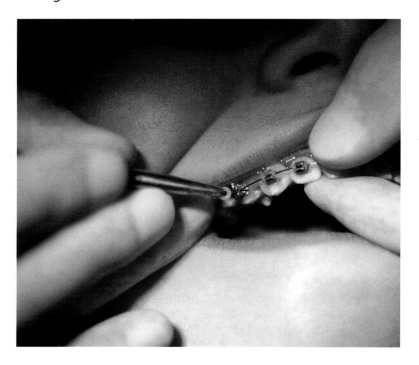

Orthodontists attach wires to the teeth.

medical necessity for improving a person's health and quality of life.

In North America, there is a tendency in the dental profession to consider anyone with crooked teeth to be in "need" of braces. This "need," however, is not necessarily a medical one. It is quite rare for a human being to grow up with perfectly straight teeth. According to some studies, more than 70 percent of North Americans have a malloclusion of some kind that could be improved by braces. Not all malloclusions, however, cause the types of dental problems discussed above. Nevertheless, if you have even a minor malloclusion, more likely than not your dentist will suggest that you get braces.

Constructing the "Perfect " Smile

A large part of why we perceive a person with crooked teeth as needing braces is due to our societal values of beauty. In North America, we are ***inundated*** with images of models, actors, and other people in the media with beautiful, perfect smiles. Most of these perfect smiles are the result of thousands of dollars worth of dental procedures and are an ideal that few people can actually achieve. Nevertheless, many of us have come to see anything less than perfectly straight, evenly spaced teeth as unacceptable, maybe even ugly. On some occasions, we may even judge other people based on the look of their teeth rather than on their personalities. When you are told that you need braces, it can sometimes be hard to figure out if you truly *need* them for medical purposes, or if you are assumed to need them for cosmetic purposes.

None of this means, however, that you should not get braces for cosmetic purposes. A person's smile can play a big part in his self-esteem, and self-esteem plays a huge role in a person's ability to interact socially and feel confident. The impact that your smile has on your self-esteem can be just as legitimate a reason to get braces as

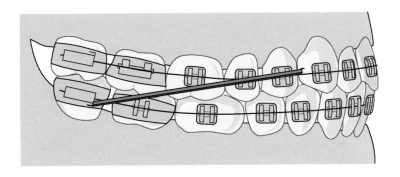

Braces pull the teeth into proper position.

87

Taking Care of Your Smile

a medical need. Braces, however, are a very expensive dental procedure. In the United States, they usually cost between $3,000 and $7,000 and are often not paid for by dental insurance, so you and your parents or guardians may have to give serious consideration to the benefits of braces before deciding to get them.

If you have braces and are thinking about locking lips, you may want to be cautious! Though the rumor about two people with braces getting locked together is usually quite false, bumping metal can be painful, and cuts on your lips can occur. Kissing is a very intimate, personal thing, so it's good to go slow anyway. When one of you has braces, slow and gentle is definitely better than hot and heavy. If you or your partner is really self-conscious about your braces, don't get too upset. Your braces won't be on forever, so there will be plenty of time for kissing in the future.

If you decide to get braces, your first step will be to have a consultation with a dentist or orthodontist. An orthodontist is someone who specializes in the treatment of misaligned teeth and jaws. In such a consultation, you may be shown photographs of other people who have had braces. Keep in mind, however, that the "before" and "after" pictures that are often shown to promote braces may not necessarily reflect the results you can expect. If someone is encouraging you to get braces to improve your looks, take note of the before and after pictures you are being shown. Is the beautiful person in the "after" picture wearing much more makeup than she was wearing in the "before" picture? Is the lighting in the "after" picture ***accentuating*** attractive features, like her eyes and cheekbones, in a way that they weren't accentuated in the "before" pictures? Is the "before" picture in black and white but the "after" picture in color? You should be aware that braces can do wonderful things, but you should also be a wise consumer and conscientious of the fact that some representations and promises may not be true to life. The important thing when considering braces is that you recognize why your dentist is encouraging you to get braces, why YOU want braces, and what braces can realistically do for you.

Having considered all of these issues, what can you expect if you, like millions of other people, do decide to get braces? If you get braces, you will most likely be visiting an orthodontist. In general, dentists and orthodontists recommend the ages between ten and fourteen as the best years for braces. It is in these years that your adult teeth are coming in but are still in early stages of development and easily ***malleable***. At this time, your jaw is usually still growing as well, and an orthodontist can use different techniques to stimulate this growth to occur in a more beneficial way. However, despite the years between ten and fourteen being optimum ages for braces, people get braces at all ages, and even large numbers of adults decide to get braces. In fact, some orthodontists estimate that as many as twenty percent of their patients are adults.

Different orthodontists have different techniques and methods for adjusting a person's teeth. As with other medical procedures, it is always a good idea to get more than one opinion before committing to braces. The method that one orthodontist favors may be drastically different from another orthodontist's and could yield very different results. Consider the following example:

Rudy was twelve years old when he and his parents decided it was time for him to get braces. He had a large overbite, and a number of his front teeth were quite crooked. Rudy's mother scheduled a consultation with an orthodontist. At the consultation, the orthodontist took X rays then mapped a plan-of-action for Rudy's treatment. He showed the X rays to Rudy and his mother so they could see how crowded the teeth were. He suggested that they remove four teeth, two from the top and two from the bottom, to make room, and then pull Rudy's top row of teeth back to meet his bottom teeth, thus eliminating the overbite.

During the consultation, the orthodontist showed Rudy a number of pictures of former patients who had successful treatment with braces. Rudy was impressed by how good everyone looked with their perfect smiles, and was soon convinced. Rudy's mother, however, was not so sure. She didn't like the idea of having so many of her son's teeth extracted, and she was suspicious of the orthodontist's photographs. She decided to take Rudy for a second opinion just in case.

Rudy's mother described the suggested procedure to the second orthodontist. The orthodontist examined Rudy then shook her head. She explained that, in her opinion, extracting teeth would have a negative effect on Rudy's facial features and perhaps a devastating effect on his self-esteem. The orthodontist explained that Rudy's overbite was due to a small, deeply set bottom jaw. She also pointed out that Rudy's nose was already quite prominent and, since he was still growing, could become more prominent in the future. The orthodontist said that, in her opinion, removing four teeth and pulling the top

Taking Care of Your Smile

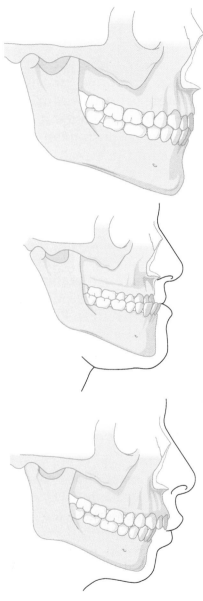

The top image shows proper tooth alignment. The middle image shows an underbite, while the lower image portrays an overbite.

teeth back would cause the bottom of Rudy's face to look like it had collapsed inward, making his nose even more prominent. The orthodontist felt certain that such a procedure could only cause disappointing results and suggested a better approach would be to insert something called a bite-plate in the hopes of stimulating the bottom jaw to grow slightly and move forward. Once this was accomplished, she would remove small amounts of enamel between the teeth and insert spacers to push Rudy's teeth apart, thereby making room for the teeth to be straightened.

As you can see from the above example, braces can have a big impact on the way that a person looks, and not all orthodontists will have the same approach. The possible changes you may experience and your orthodontist's professional reputation both need to be considered carefully. Many young people have additional concerns like feeling self-conscious about their braces. They may worry about things like people laughing at them, not being able to eat the foods they like, whether they can still perform the same activities (like playing instruments or sports), how long they will need to have the braces on, and whether they can kiss with braces.

> Some famous actors who have had braces include Tom Cruise, Cameron Diaz, Whoopi Goldberg, and Ashley Judd. Some famous sports figures who have worn braces include Marina Hingis, Venus and Serena Williams, Hardy Nickerson, Terrell Davis, and Brett Farve. Singers who have donned the "metal mouth" include Cher, Diana Ross, Chris Kirkpatrick, Gwen Steffani, and Monica.

93

Taking Care of Your Smile

For the most part, you are able to do all the same things, like playing instruments, sports, and eating foods you like, that you did before having braces. However, here and there, some adjustments do have to be made. For example, because some parts of your braces are sharp and can cut the soft tissues of your mouth, you may need to exercise more caution when playing sports. Playing a wind instrument may also take some adjustment while you get used to the feeling of having the braces in your mouth. Bigger changes may be necessary when it comes to foods. Although you can still eat most of the foods you ate prior to getting braces, you will need to cut hard foods, like apples and carrots, into small pieces so that they don't damage your braces. Similarly, you should give up hard, sticky, or chewy candies as they can very easily damage the wires of your braces.

As for the issue of people laughing at you for having braces, today so many people have braces that you probably don't need to worry. Furthermore, braces have improved a lot in the past few decades, and today some braces are clear and hardly visible. However, if you are afraid of experiencing stressful social situations because of your braces, you may want to consider how you will deal with the situation before the situation actually arises. This way, you can be prepared. For example, you may wish to point out the recent trend towards braces in Hollywood. Many people also find humor to be a good way of dissolving uncomfortable social situations and dealing with the awkwardness braces can cause.

Proper dental care, as was discussed in chapter 2, is even more important when you have braces because the braces create additional places where food, bacteria, and acid can get trapped and held next to your teeth. Cleaning your teeth when you have braces may require some more specialized equipment than your normal tooth-

Constructing the "Perfect " Smile

Many adolescents have braces today.

Taking Care of Your Smile

If you wanted to have all thirty-two of your teeth resurfaced and were paying $750 per veneer, you would end up paying $24,000! That's more than some people pay for their cars. If you paid the high-end price of $2,000 per veneer, your total bill would be $64,000. That's more than some people pay for a house and more than the average North American earns in a year! It's easy to see why most people only get veneers for the teeth that are most visible.

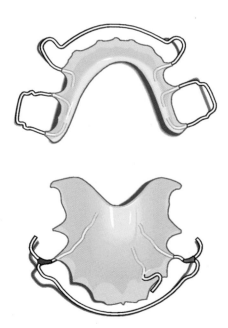

Retainers are other devices orthodontists may use to correct tooth alignment.

brush and dental floss. Your orthodontist will probably give you a narrow, hook-like brush for brushing between the wires and your teeth. Your orthodontist may also give you a tool for threading dental floss more easily between your teeth. Keeping your teeth clean when you have braces does take more care and time, but it is extremely important. When you finally get your braces off, you want your teeth to be in better, not worse, condition than they were before you got the braces put on. In most cases, after your braces have been removed, you will have to continue wearing a wire or plastic retainer for a period of time specified by your orthodontist. This retainer helps your teeth maintain the shape that you and your braces worked so hard to achieve.

Tooth Contouring and Reshaping

In Rudy's story, you read that one of the procedures the orthodontist recommended besides braces was removing some enamel. Enamel is the protective layer of your teeth, so it may sound scary if someone suggests removing it, but strategically removing very small amounts of enamel to improve the spacing and shape of a person's teeth is part of a common procedure called tooth contouring and reshaping.

Tooth contouring and reshaping is a precise procedure in which files, abrasive strips, and sometimes lasers and computer imaging are used to make subtle adjustments to a tooth's size and shape. The amounts of enamel removed in this process are necessarily small, as removing too much enamel would cause permanent damage to your teeth. Nevertheless, if done skillfully and properly, these small adjustments can make a big difference to the overall appearance of your teeth.

To be eligible for tooth contouring and reshaping, your teeth must be in good health. If your teeth are already weak, the reshaping process could cause damage or breakage. If your enamel is too thin, the process could expose dentine or even the sensitive pulp. X rays will be taken before the procedure begins to locate the area of the pulp inside the tooth. Tooth contouring is often combined with resurfacing techniques.

Porcelain Veneers

Today, braces are not the only way to achieve that straight-toothed smile. In recent years, porcelain veneers have become more and more popular as an alternative to braces. In this process, a dentist or orthodontist makes a model of your teeth. This model is used as a basis for designing thin shells that will cover the fronts of your teeth. Porcelain veneers are attractive to many people because they correct a wide range of problems, from gaps, crooked teeth, and stains, to minor chips, and cracks. Furthermore, porcelain veneers can be put on quickly (the process takes just three appointments) and can eliminate the lengthy, uncomfortable process of braces. Veneers have helped many people who suffer poor self-esteem because of stained or irregular teeth and have restored many accident victims' smiles. However, if you are considering porcelain veneers, you should keep in mind that the process cannot be reversed once it is begun. This is because some of your enamel must be removed to

make room for the new porcelain shell that will go on your tooth. Once this enamel is removed, your tooth is forever changed and will never look correct again without a porcelain veneer.

Another real drawback to porcelain veneers is their cost. In the United States, the average cost of a single porcelain veneer can be anywhere from $750 to $2,000. Largely because of cost, veneers are usually only placed on the top six front teeth. To have veneers placed on these teeth alone, however, can cost from $4,500 to $12,000. Orthodontists do tend to charge less per veneer if you are having a number of them done. Nevertheless, the cost can be astounding and well beyond what many people can afford. Veneers are usually placed on sets of teeth rather than on just one tooth because it would be difficult to make one veneer match the color and size of all your other teeth.

Another consideration is that the veneers are not permanent and must eventually be replaced. With proper care, your veneers could last more than ten years, but they can't last forever. Furthermore, porcelain is relatively easy to crack, chip, or break. Broken veneers will need replacement and could lead to some hefty dental bills. If cost is a serious concern for you, you should be aware that there are other, cheaper materials that veneers can be made out of, but they may not last as long, be as stain resistant, or look as natural as porcelain. It is also good to keep in mind that, though the porcelain is quite stain resistant, the cement used to glue the porcelain to your teeth is not. Things like coffee, tea, red wine, and smoking will stain any cement poking out around the edges of the veneers. The veneers themselves, and bacteria and plaque that collect at the edges of the veneers, can cause gum irritation, disease, and *recession*. As with braces, good oral hygiene is extremely important.

Many people who have damaged teeth would like the benefits of porcelain veneers but are not eligible for the procedure. This is because your tooth needs a certain amount of strength to support a veneer. Veneers can only be adhered to tooth enamel, so even though some of your enamel will be removed, there still must be enough left to accomplish the procedure. A tooth that is badly damaged by decay, stripped enamel, or breakage, or that has a filling, will not be a good candidate for a veneer. Furthermore, if you have gum disease, you may not be able to get veneers.

Gold, Porcelain, and Combination Crowns

If you have significant damage to your teeth, or wish to improve the look of your teeth but are not a candidate for tooth contouring or veneers, your dentist may suggest that you get crowns. Crowns help to stabilize the structure of a damaged tooth and can be both medical and cosmetic.

Whereas a veneer is a shell that is affixed just to the front of your tooth, a crown is like a hard glove that fits snugly over your entire tooth. Gold crowns are usually used in the molars and back teeth. Gold crowns fit closely to your remaining tooth material, protect your tooth from further damage, and are permanent and effective. The drawback to gold crowns, however, is that they cannot be made to look like natural teeth. Most peo-

ple who need a front tooth capped would prefer a non-metal material.

Like veneers, crowns can also be made out of porcelain. This is the type of crown that people generally use for front or highly visible teeth. Like veneers, porcelain crowns can work wonders for restoring a person's smile. The problem with porcelain crowns, however, is that they are not as durable as gold and are more susceptible to cracking and chipping. Furthermore, whereas gold bonds firmly to your remaining tooth and allows much of the original tooth to be saved, porcelain crowns usually require that most of the remaining tooth be removed to make room for the porcelain crown and don't fit as snugly. Porcelain crowns, like veneers, have a tendency to irritate gums and can cause gum disease and recession. Porcelain crowns are also much more expensive than gold crowns.

> Tooth crowns can cost anywhere between $500 and $3,500 dollars per crown. That's an expensive tooth!

A third option available is porcelain fused to a metal crown. Combination crowns are metal on the inside, which allows them to bond more closely to your remaining tooth, but have a porcelain coating on the outside. This type of crown has the structural benefits of metal crowns, but looks more like a real tooth. Combination crowns still do not look as much like real teeth as porcelain crowns do, but many people find them to be a great visual improvement over gold.

Braces, tooth contouring and reshaping, porcelain veneers, and tooth crowns are some of the major techniques for constructing "perfect," even-toothed smiles, but they are not the only techniques out there. If you are concerned about the shape or arrangement of your teeth, you can discuss these techniques and others with your dentist or orthodontist.

6
DENTAL CARE AND YOUR FUTURE

Wisdom teeth are the last teeth a person will get. These are the very last four molars in your mouth. Sometime between the ages of seventeen and twenty-one, these teeth will erupt, which means that they push through the surface of the gum. Often this can be painful, but that does not necessarily mean there is problem. For some people, wisdom teeth fit neatly into the back of their mouths. Other people never get wisdom teeth at all.

Your Wisdom Teeth—Should They Stay or Should They Go?

Many people, however, are not lucky enough to have their wisdom teeth come in problem-free. What often happens is that a wisdom tooth becomes impacted. What this means is that the tooth fails to erupt properly. Mesial impaction means that the wisdom tooth is angled forward. If you were to open your mouth and look at the tooth, you would probably only see a very small part of the crown. A distal impaction happens when the tooth is angled toward the back of the mouth. A vertical or horizontal impaction is also possible. In these impactions, none of the crown is likely to be visible. In the case of vertical impaction, the tooth is upright under the gum, but its situation is too far under the gum line. If a wisdom tooth is horizontally impacted, it lies parallel to the surface of the gum and points toward the front of the mouth. These impacts can be categorized still further. When a tooth has not penetrated through the jawbone, it is called a bony impaction. This differs from a soft tissue impaction, where a tooth might have penetrated successfully through the jawbone, but has not yet done so through the gums. Impactions can be painful and can necessitate removal of the wisdom teeth.

106

The most common cause of impactions is a lack of space in the jaws to accommodate these final teeth. Why is it that so many people do not have enough room in their mouth for these teeth? Some people think this problem is actually a result of the better hygiene and overall dental health we enjoy today. In the past, due to abrasive foods and poor dental hygiene, a person would typically have already lost some teeth by the time his wisdom teeth began to erupt. Since some teeth were already missing, there was probably room for the new wisdom teeth. Today, however, not only are human beings likely to still have most or all of their teeth by the time they hit their late teens and early twenties, but their teeth are likely to be healthier, less worn, and as a result bigger. In short, good dental health has caused there to be less room in the mouths of modern human beings.

When wisdom teeth are only partially erupted, gum infections can occur. The gum around the crown is not

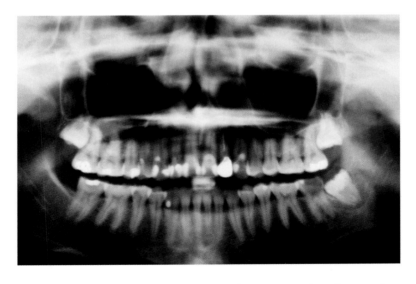

Dentists often use X rays to determine the position of wisdom teeth.

107

attached to the tooth. When a person eats, food particles can enter this tiny pocket of space. The food then sits there and rots, bacteria flourish, and the tooth eventually decays. It is impossible for the person to brush the pocket, since it is below the surface of the gum. Along with the problem of decay comes the related problem of bad breath. Even if wisdom teeth erupt well, the position of the wisdom teeth can make them difficult to clean. Sometimes, especially in the case of mesial impaction, the wisdom teeth touch their neighbors, which can create an additional place for food particles to be lodged. Plaque then builds up and decay occurs. For these reasons, it is quite common for people to have their wisdom teeth removed.

Since many of these impacts happen below the surface, it is necessary to have a dentist assess whether your wisdom teeth will have to be removed. A dentist might

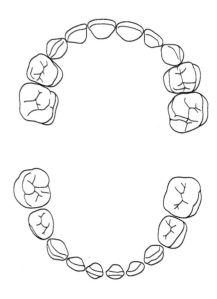

Children have twenty baby teeth.

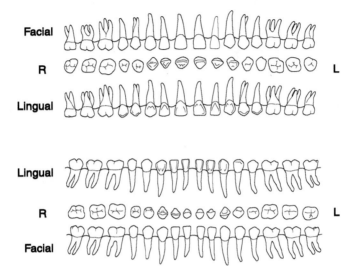

An adult with wisdom teeth will have sixteen teeth on top and sixteen teeth on the bottom.

suggest to you that X rays be taken of your mouth to better picture exactly what is going on. Sometimes, a dentist will simply monitor the situation, making sure that the wisdom teeth are coming in properly.

Having your wisdom teeth removed can pose a number of risks. When a tooth is extracted, the socket left behind does not always heal properly. If a blood clot does not form (a condition known as a dry socket), the healing can be delayed. Damage to nerves, while rare, can also occur. When a nerve is damaged or bruised during an extraction, it is called *paresthesia*. Both these complications occur less frequently in young people, which is one reason why it is often recommended by dentists that problematic wisdom teeth be removed as soon as possible.

109

Taking Care of Your Smile

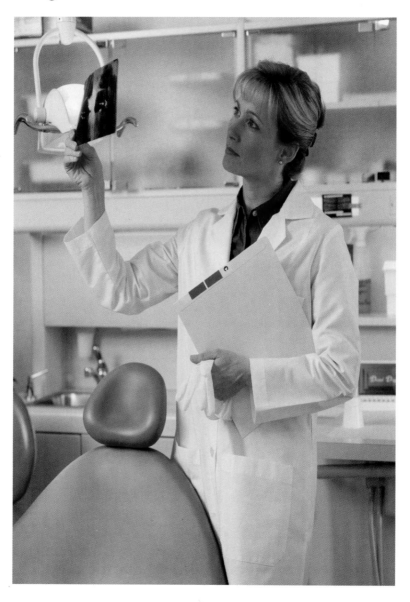

Many dentists refer to X rays to assess dental health.

The Health of Your Mouth and Your Heart

Did you know that having a healthy mouth can also help you have a healthy heart? This may sound strange, but recent scientific evidence has linked periodontal diseases like gingivitis with heart disease. But how could a disease of the gums affect your heart?

As you now know, there are bacteria present in your mouth all the time, and these bacteria cause plaque on your teeth. Your mouth, however, is not the only place in your body where plaque occurs. You also have plaque that builds up in your veins and arteries. You are constantly swallowing the bacteria that reside in your mouth. Scientists now believe that these swallowed bacteria enter the blood stream and attach to the plaques in blood. These plaques travel in your veins and arteries

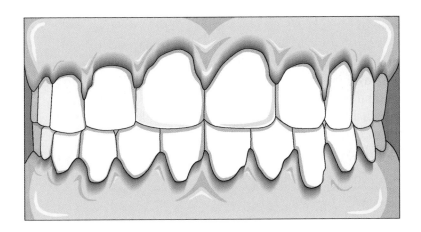

Gingivitis causes inflammation of the gums.

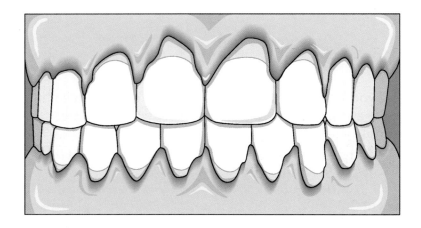

Periodontitis is a more serious gum disease than gingivitis.

and can form blood clots. The plaques are worsened by the presence of the bacteria. When a blood clot forms in the arteries of your heart and stops the blood flow, it causes a heart attack. When a similar sort of thing happens in your brain, it causes a stroke.

Even if you don't care very much about the health of your teeth, you probably care very much about the health of your heart. The newly discovered links to heart disease are just one more reason to brush and floss every day and to visit your dentist twice a year. Since your risk of heart disease increases as you age, the need for good dental hygiene is even more important as you get older.

According to some studies, people with periodontal disease are at twice the risk of developing heart disease.

INJURIES

As children, many people experienced chipping their teeth or even knocking one a bit loose. Toddlers, since they are learning how to walk—and often learning to do it by running everywhere!—lose their teeth more than older children do. For children, falls are a major cause of losing teeth.

> Dentists estimate that mouth guards prevent at least 200,000 tooth injuries in high school football players every year.

As we get older, however, different things are more apt to cause injury to our teeth. Many teenagers and adults experience tooth injuries from things like sports and car accidents. These are called traumatic injuries of the teeth. Teenagers often have active lifestyles, with much of their free time taken up by organized sports. Something like a car accident cannot always be helped, but losing teeth while playing sports often can. Mouth guards should be used during many sports, and are often requirements of the game. In some organized sports, like football and hockey, the risk of tooth and other facial damage is so great that instead of simply wearing mouth guards, people wear face masks. The dangers to your teeth in some sports seem obvious. A quick look at a team of professional hockey players reveals a lot of toothless grins. Many professional hockey players wear dentures, despite still being young adults! There are other sports, however, where the dangers to your smile might not seem so obvious. Baseball, field hockey, basketball,

Taking Care of Your Smile

Wearing a protective face mask can prevent tooth injuries.

114

skateboarding, in-line skating, and others are all activities in which mouth guards or face masks should be worn.

> At least three million people are treated for traumatic facial injuries in the United States every year.

If you've injured a tooth, you should not delay in going to a dentist or a doctor. A loosened tooth is generally not a dental emergency and will typically heal in approximately three days. Nevertheless, it is best to have a dentist evaluate the situation before assuming that a loose tooth is no big deal. If you have damaged the surface of a tooth, you should also consult your dentist. Sometimes a chip to a tooth might be small with no pain and hardly any visible sign of damage. In such a case, a person might decide not to go to the dentist. However, the extent of such injuries is not always immediately apparent. When a tooth is cracked or broken, it is more susceptible to further damage from acid attacks and decay. The injury should be treated as soon as possible to prevent damage from spreading and worsening. Even if the injury seems very minor, it is best to get treatment quickly before complications or decay can set in.

> Athletes who don't wear mouth guards are sixty times more likely to sustain injuries to their teeth than athletes who do.

When a tooth is knocked out, it is a dental emergency. Before you do anything else, you should rinse the tooth with clean water and press it back into the hole. This will keep the blood vessels and nerves connected to their

blood supply so that they do not die. You must then proceed immediately to a dentist or to a hospital. The tooth
must be replaced within fifteen minutes if it is going to
take hold again and be saved.

Oral Cancer

Oral cancer, or cancer of the mouth, is another health
concern to be aware of as you age. Cancer comes from
genes mutating in cells. These mutated genes cause the
affected cells to grow uncontrollably. They are unable to
repair themselves and do not die. These mutations can
be brought on by a number of factors including exposure
to chemicals. The lifestyle choices that people make
when they are young can increase their risk of developing cancer later in life. The use of any type of tobacco, including cigarettes, pipes, cigars, and chewing tobacco,
greatly increases your risk for getting oral cancer as well
as many other types of cancer. People who drink alcohol
excessively also have a greater chance of getting oral cancer. Exposure to sunlight, and dangerous UV radiation, is
another cause of cancer of the mouth.

Unfortunately, oral cancer often goes undiscovered
until it has progressed to an advanced stage, and the
longer it goes untreated, the less chance a person has of
survival. It most commonly occurs on the lips, tongue, or
floor of the mouth, but it can occur in other oral tissues
as well. Knowing how to identify oral cancer, and
whether or not you are it risk for contracting it, can help
to identify the cancer when it is still in its early stages.
One of the problems with oral cancer, however, is that in
its early stages it is difficult to notice. Sometimes there is
no pain associated with this cancer, so it can develop

quietly and unnoticed. Dentists and doctors, however, are trained to recognize the warning signs, so regular dental checkups are an important part of prevention. Sometimes the cancer appears as a red or white patch and can look like a canker sore. Canker sores, red patches, and white spots, however, are pretty common sights in the human mouth, and you

> Only about half of all people diagnosed with oral cancer will survive more than five years after diagnosis.

don't want to panic every time you see one of these manifestations. A good rule of thumb is that if the sore or discolored patch remains for more than fourteen days, you should have it checked by a professional. Other signs of oral cancer include lumps, pain or numbness, and difficulty speaking, swallowing and chewing.

Will I Lose My Teeth When I Get Old?

Many people believe that getting older automatically means losing their teeth. This is not necessarily the case. As you have seen, much of whether you will keep your teeth as you age has to do with what happened to your teeth when you were young. If you had poor early childhood nutrition, or if you have a genetic **predisposition** towards dental disease and tooth loss, there may be little you can do to prevent losing your teeth. However, you live in an age where you benefit from better food, better hygiene products, better education, and better dentistry

Healthy teeth play a vital role in your overall well-being.

than ever before. Today there are many reasons for your teeth to be strong and healthy and to remain so as you age.

Your mouth is the site of so many pleasures in life. You eat with it, speak with it, smile, laugh, and kiss with it.

Dental Care and Your Future

Keeping your mouth healthy should be a top priority. If you do your job well, your teeth will respond. If you brush, floss, and visit your dentist regularly, you'll keep on smiling for the rest of your life.

Bonner, Michael P. and Earl L. Mindell. *The Oral Health Bible*. North Bergen, N.J.: Basic Health Publications, 2003.

Christen, Arden G. and Jennifer A. Klein. *Tobacco and Your Oral Health*. Chicago: Quintessence Publishing, 1997.

Lee, McHenry, Joleen Jackson, Bicki J. Audette, and McHenry "Mac" Lee. *Nothin' Personal Doc, But I Hate Dentists!: The Feel Good Guide to Going to the Dentist*. Copperas Cove, Tex.: IHD Publishing, 1999.

Ring, Malvin E. *Dentistry: An Illustrated History*. New York: Harry N. Abrams, 1992 (reprint addition).

Schissel, Marvin J. and John E. Dodes. *Healthy Teeth: A User's Manual: Everything You Need to Know to Find a Good Dentist and Take Proper Care of Your Teeth*. New York: Griffin Trade Paperback, 1999.

Scully, Crispian. *ABC of Oral Health*. London, U.K.: BMJ Books, 2001.

Silverstein, Alvin, Virginia B. Silverstein, Laura Silverstein Nunn, and Mark Frankland. *Tooth Decay and Cavities*. Danbury, Conn.: Franklin Watts, 1999.

Taintor, Jerry F., and Mary Jane Taintor. *The Complete Guide to Better Dental Care*. New York: Checkmark Books, 1999.

Wynbrandt, James. *The Excruciating History of Dentistry: Toothsome Tales and Oral Oddities from Babylon To Braces*. New York: Griffin Trade Paperback, 2000.

FOR MORE INFORMATION

Academy of General Dentistry
www.agd.org

American Academy of Pediatric Dentistry
www.aapd.org

American Academy of Periodontology
www.perio.org

American Association of Oral and Maxillofacial Surgeons
www.aaoms.org

American Association of Orthodontists
www.braces.org

American Dental Association
www.ada.org

Animated-Teth.com
www.animated-teeth.com

Canadian Academy of Periodontology
www.cap-acp.ca

Canadian Association of Oral and Maxillofacial Surgeons
www.caoms.com

Canadian Association of Orthodontists
www.cao-aco.org

Canadian Association of Public Health Dentistry
www.caphd-acsdp.org

Canadian Dental Association
www.cda-adc.ca

Dental Related Internet Resources
www.dental-resources.com

Flossing
www.floss.com

Publisher's note:
The Web sites listed on these pages were active at the time of publication. The publisher is not responsible for Web sites that have
changed their addresses or discontinued operation since the date of
publication. The publisher will review and update the Web sites
upon each reprint.

abrasive Causing irritation.

accentuating (ak-SEN-choo-ate-ing) Accenting, emphasizing; also, intensifying.

caries A progressive destruction of bone or tooth, especially tooth decay.

cavities Areas of decay in a tooth.

chromosomes The DNA-containing bodies of cells that contain all or most of an individual's genes.

collective dentition The development and cutting of all the teeth.

conquistadors (con-KEES-tuh-doors) Conquerors, specifically leaders in the Spanish conquest of America and especially of Mexico and Peru in the sixteenth century.

cosmetic Relating to that which makes for beauty, especially of the complexion.

cumulative Increasing in severity because of repeated exposure.

DNA Any of various nucleic acids that are usually the molecular basis of heredity, which are found especially in cell nuclei, and are constructed of a double helix.

fervor Intensity of feeling or expression.

forceps An instrument for grasping, holding firmly, or exerting traction upon objects, especially for delicate operations.

genes Specific sequences of nucleotides in DNA or RNA that are located in the germ plasm usually on a chromosome and that are the functional units of inheritance.

gingiva (JIN-juh-vuh) Gum.

grafted Implanted (living tissue) surgically.

inhibitor An agent that slows or interferes with a chemical action.

inundated Covered with a flood; overflowed; over-

123

whelmed.

malleable Capable of being extended, shaped, or otherwise influenced.

mummified Embalmed and dried as a body treated for burial with preservatives in the manner of the ancient Egyptians.

neutralizes Makes chemically neutral, neither acid nor basic.

predisposition Inclination; susceptibility.

premature Happening, arriving, existing, or performed before the proper, usual, or intended time.

prenatal Occurring, existing, or performed before birth.

rationally Reasonably; agreeably, with understanding.

rations Shares, especially as determined by supplies.

recession To withdraw or move back.

systemic Relating to or common to a system, so that it affects the body generally.

therapeutic Of or relating to the treatment of disease or disorders by remedial agents or methods.

topical Designed for or involving local application and action (as on the body's skin).

trajectory A path, progression, or line of development resembling a physical trajectory, which is a curve that a body (as a planet or comet in its orbit or a rocket) describes in space.

INDEX

PICTURE CREDITS

BIOGRAPHIES

Autumn Libal received her degree from Smith College in Northampton, Massachusetts. A former water-aerobics instructor, she now dedicates herself exclusively to writing for young people. Other Mason Crest series she has contributed to include PSYCHIATRIC DISORDERS: DRUGS & PSYCHOLOGY FOR THE MIND AND BODY and YOUTH WITH SPECIAL NEEDS. She has also written health-related articles for *New Moon: The Magazine for Girls and Their Dreams*.

Chris Hovius is a graduate of Queen's University in Kingston, Ontario. He is a freelance author who lives in Vancouver, British Columbia.

Dr. Sara Forman graduated from Barnard College and Harvard Medical School. She completed her residency in Pediatrics at Children's Hospital of Philadelphia and a fellowship in Adolescent Medicine at Children's Hospital Boston (CHB). She currently is an attending in Adolescent Medicine at CHB, where she has served as Director of the Adolescent Outpatient Eating Disorders Program for the past nine years. She has also consulted for the National Eating Disorder Screening Project on its high school initiative and has presented at many conferences about teens and eating disorders. In addition to her clinical and administrative roles in the Eating Disorders Program, Dr. Forman teaches medical students and residents and coordinates the Adolescent Medicine rotation at CHB. Dr. Forman sees primary care adolescent patients in the Adolescent Clinic at CHB, at Bentley College, and at the Germaine Lawrence School, a residential school for emotionally disturbed teenage girls.

Nancy Noyes is a child psychiatric nurse practitioner in psychopharmacology at both Boston Children's Hospital and University Health Care for Kids in Portland, Maine. Nancy's husband Bill is a dentist and she is also quite familiar with the dental field and dental health education. Nancy received her BSN from West Virigina University Medical Center, her MS from the University of New Hampshire, and her certificate of advanced studies from Northeastern University.